Now Playing

Learning Mythology through Film

D0580231

Gail Rosen
Eva M. Thury
Margaret K. Devinney

New York   Oxford
Oxford University Press

Oxford University Press, Inc., publishes works that further Oxford University s
objective of excellence in research, scholarship, and education.

Oxford New York
Auckland Cape Town Dar es Salaam Hong Kong Karachi
Kuala Lumpur Madrid Melbourne Mexico City Nairobi
New Delhi Shanghai Taipei Toronto

With offices in
Argentina Austria Brazil Chile Czech Republic France Greece
Guatemala Hungary Italy Japan Poland Portugal Singapore
South Korea Switzerland Thailand Turkey Ukraine Vietnam

For titles covered by Section 112 of the U.S. Higher
Education Opportunity Act, please visit
www.oup.com/us/he for the latest information about
pricing and alternate formats.

Published by Oxford University Press, Inc.
198 Madison Avenue, New York, New York 10016
http://www.oup.com

ISBN: 978-0-19-986277-1

Printing number: 9 8 7 6 5 4 3 2

Printed in the United States of America
on acid-free paper

CONTENTS

Introduction

Films provide much more than entertainment. They often reflect the values, beliefs, and concerns of their audience, and can provide valuable insights to students of mythology. They can also be used to enhance students' understanding of challenging subject matter, facilitate class discussion, and foster an energetic and exciting atmosphere in the classroom. This film supplement, new to the third edition, covers 30 films and three episodes from contemporary television series. Each entry in the supplement contains references to specific chapters in *Introduction to Mythology, Third Edition,* to enable smooth integration of the supplement with the fascinating and wide-ranging ideas in the book.

The information in the supplement facilitates discussion about either an entire film or one or more short scenes in a film. Each entry includes recommended clips with a time and minute counter. These clips can stand alone or be used in combination, if viewing the entire film is not practical. Data about producers, directors, and actors are included in each entry. This will enable students and instructors to locate the films, as well as criticism about them. The supplement also provides background information as well as a synopsis. This will allows instructors and students unfamiliar with the film to make an informed decision about which films to use. This will also help to compare and contrast the different versions of stories that evolve from the myths as well as identify central ideas within them. Each entry also includes questions that can start a class discussion or inspire written assignments. Suggested answers are provided in the Instructor's version. These answers emphasize important elements of each film and suggest connections to the material in *Introduction to Mythology.*

The films discussed in the supplement are from time periods ranging from 1948 to 2011. Included are films from places such as Indonesia, Brazil, and others, as well as the United States. The films used are critically acclaimed, animated, musicals, and big-budget adventures as well as low-budget gems. Some tell familiar stories in new ways, some explore mythological concepts in surprising ways, and some combine contemporary stories with ancient traditions. Some of these films reached a wide audience while others may be unfamiliar to many. All contain moments of beauty, and all teach something useful about mythology and provide new and different perspectives on fascinating material.

It is hoped that this supplement will be useful and enjoyable, and will enable the discovery of new and exciting films and the rediscovery of familiar favorites.

1. Beauty and the Beast (La belle et la bête)

Film Data

Year: 1946

Director: Jean Cocteau

Length: 96 minutes

Rated: NA

Characters/Actors

Jean Marais: La Bête (The Beast)/The Prince/Avenant

Josette Day: Belle

Mila Parély: Félicie

Nane Germon: Adélaïde

Michel Auclair: Ludovic

Raoul Marco: The Usurer

Marcel André: Belle's Father

Connection to Chapters

Chapter 34. Applying Theory: How to Perform a Jungian Analysis

Chapter 37. Germany: Grimms' *Household Tales*

Recommended Scenes

The scene of the introduction with the text occurs at 00:02:32 through 00:03:35.

The scene of Belle's father entering the castle and making the deal with the Beast occurs at 00:17:05 through 00:24:55.

The scene of Belle's initial encounter with the beast occurs at 00:36:20 through 00:40:30.

The scene of the Beast drinking from Belle's hands occurs at 00:49:50.

The scene of the Beast asking Belle's forgiveness occurs at 00:54:47.

The scene of Belle attempting to give her sisters jewels occurs at 01:06:48.

The scene of Belle's love saving the beast and the resolution of the story occurs at 01:25:15.

Viewing Information

The French film (with English subtitles) *Beauty and the Beast* is the work of acclaimed filmmaker Jean Cocteau. *Beauty and the Beast* is loosely based on a tale by Jeanne-Marie Leprince de Beaumont, although you may recognize some elements from both *Beauty and the Beast* and *Cinderella*. This film was made for adults, and differs from the more contemporary children's films of this tale. *Beauty and the Beast* will provide an excellent way to discuss the layers of meaning in the household tales, as well as Jung's and Rank's ideas pertaining to household tales.

Synopsis

Lovely Belle (Day) is treated like a servant by her two mean sisters, who believe they are too beautiful to work. When Avenant (Marais) proposes to Belle, she refuses because she wants to stay with her debt-ridden father. After failing to resolve his financial affairs, Belle's father (André) gets lost in the forest and finds himself in a creepy castle. He takes a rose for Belle and incurs the wrath of the Beast (Marais). The Beast says he will kill him unless one of his daughters agrees to die in his place. When Belle learns of this, she sneaks away to the Beast's castle in order to save her father's life. But the Beast treats Belle very well and dines with her at seven o'clock each night. Each night he proposes marriage and Belle refuses. Belle finds the Beast repulsive, but sees he has a good heart. The Beast allows Belle to visit her ailing father and she promises to return within a week. Belle heals her father when she returns home. But Belle's sisters are jealous of Belle because of the riches the Beast bestowed on Belle. They trick Belle into staying with them and plan to steal the Beast's riches. They convince Avenant and their bother Ludovic (Auclair) to rescue Belle and help steal the Beast's treasures. When Belle realizes the Beast is dying, she returns to him. Avenant is shot and turns into a beast, and the Beast transforms into a handsome man who looks like Avenant. The former Beast says he was saved by a loving look from Belle. She also loves him, and becomes his Queen. The film ends as they happily float away.

3

1. Explain how the film reflects the values and ethics of the time period when it was made.

2. Describe the ways that the film, like the stories of the Grimm Brothers, is directed primarily at adults.

3. Describe how the film portrays traditional values.

2. Black Orpheus (Orfeu Negro)

Film Data

Year: 1959

Director: Marcel Camus

Length: 100 minutes

Rated: PG

Characters/Actors

Breno Mello:	Orfeo
Marpessa Dawn:	Eurydice
Marcel Camus:	Ernesto
Fausto Guerzoni:	Fausto
Lourdes de Oliveira:	Mira
Léa Garcia:	Serafina
Ademar Da Silva:	Death
Alexandro Constantino:	Hermes

Connection to Chapters

Chapter 44. Poetry and Myth

Recommended Scenes

The scene of Mira saying she is not interested in old stories occurs at 00:014:45.

The scene of Orpheus meeting Eurydice occurs at 00:29:00 through 00:32:45.

The scene of Orpheus and Eurydice fighting and stopping death occurs at 00:47:34.

The scene of Eurydice's death occurs at 01:20:05

The scene of Orpheus searching for Eurydice at the hospital and the police station occurs at 01:24:14 through 01:28:58.

The scene of Orpheus and the janitor who helps him occurs at 01:30:10 through 01:32:10.

The scene of Orpheus contacting Eurydice at the ceremony occurs at 01:36:36 through 01:38:51.

Viewing Information

Black Orpheus is in Portuguese with English subtitles. It won an Academy Award in 1960. *Black Orpheus* features the wonderful music of acclaimed musician Antonio Carlos Jobim. The film provides a nice way to discuss the ways myths are adapted to reflect the concerns of audiences of varying places and time periods.

Synopsis

This modern interpretation of the myth of Orpheus and Eurydice is set in Rio de Janeiro, days before Carnival. It features a mostly black cast. Orpheus (Mello) is a street car conductor and a musician. His guitar playing and singing are said to make the sun rise. Orpheus is engaged to mean and controlling Mira (Oliveira), but he seems reluctant to marry her and continues to flirt with other women. This changes when Orpheus quickly falls in love with Eurydice (Dawn), a shy girl visiting her cousin Serafina (Garcia). Eurydice says she is being chased by a man who is trying to kill her. As the characters dance at Carnival, a masked and costumed figure that looks like Death (Da Silva) chases Eurydice. Orpheus tries to rescue her, but Eurydice is electrocuted on a wire while Death looks on. Orpheus refuses to believe that Eurydice is dead. He searches for her in a hospital and police station, and is finally directed to the missing persons department. There, Orpheus meets a janitor who takes him to a place guarded by a barking dog named Cerberus. Orpheus participates in a ceremony to contact the dead and hears the voice of Eurydice. She tells him he can only hear her if he does not look back. He does look back and she tells him she will be lost to him forever. Orpheus retrieves Eurydice's body from the morgue and lovingly carries her to a hill. A stone thrown by an angry Mira hits him, and Orpheus and Eurydice fall from the hill. The film ends with the little boys who have been following Orpheus throughout the film playing Orpheus's guitar and singing. A little girl joins them and dances, as they make the sun rise.

1. Explain how the film uses the myth to reflect the current concerns of its time and place.

2. Describe how the film interprets the myth to reflect the changing tastes and expectations of its audience.

3. Buffy the Vampire Slayer, "The Gift"

Film Data

Year: 2001, Season 5, episode 22

Director: Joss Whedon

Length: 44 minutes

Rated: TV/PG

Characters/Actors

Sarah Michelle Gellar:	Buffy Summers
Nicholas Brendon:	Xander Harris
Alyson Hannigan:	Willow Rosenberg
Emma Caulfield:	Anya
Michelle Trachtenberg:	Dawn Summers
James Marsters:	Spike
Anthony Head:	Rupert Giles
Clare Kramer:	Glory
Charlie Weber:	Ben

Connection to Chapters

Chapter 15. Theory: Joseph Campbell, *The Hero with a Thousand Faces* (Dave Whomsley)

Chapter 39. Applying Theory: Highlighting Different Aspects of the Same Tale Using Multiple Analyses

Chapter 43. The Vampire as Hero: Tales of the Undead in a Contemporary Context

Recommended Scenes

The opening scene of Buffy killing a vampire occurs at the start of the episode through 00:02:34.

The scene of Anya giving Buffy the magical hammer occurs at 00:08:57.

The scene of Giles explaining the ritual to Buffy occurs at 00:11:51 through 00:12:19.

The scene of Glory explaining the ritual to Dawn occurs at 00:27:00.

The scene of Buffy telling Giles she will not kill Dawn occurs at 00:13:40 through 00:15:22.

The scene of Buffy sparing Ben and Giles killing Ben occurs at 00:36:01 through 00:37:41.

The scene of Buffy sacrificing herself by jumping off the tower occurs at 00:37:55 through the end of the episode.

Viewing Information

The premise of *Buffy the Vampire Slayer* is that in every generation, one girl is chosen to fight the vampires and evil in the world. That girl is helped by an adult who is called the Watcher. Buffy (Gellar) is the chosen girl, and Giles (Head) is her watcher. Buffy is also helped by a group of friends. The episode provides an excellent way to discuss Joseph Campbell and the hero's journey. Buffy is an excellent and unusual example of a female hero. "The Gift" should provide an enjoyable way to analyze and apply Campbell's ideas to a somewhat contemporary work.

Synopsis

In Season 5 of *Buffy the Vampire Slayer,* Buffy must battle Glory (Kramer), a fallen god, who shares a body with a human doctor, Ben (Weber). In "The Gift," the Season 5 finale, Glory has taken Buffy's sister, Dawn (Trachtenberg). Dawn was created with mystical energy, and her blood, when used in a specific ritual, will open the door between dimensions. The evil Glory wants to perform this ritual and bleed Dawn, so Glory can return to another evil dimension and once again become a god. Buffy learns that if the ritual is started, the only way to stop it and save humanity will be to kill Dawn. Buffy tells Giles and her friends that she will not kill Dawn or let anyone else do so. Buffy, Willow (Hannigan), Xander (Brendon), Spike (Marsters), and Anya (Caulfield) work together to stop Glory. They defeat Glory, but the ritual has been started. Dawn offers to kill herself to stop the dimensions from bleeding together, but Buffy stops her. Buffy realizes that she can jump off the tower and stop the destruction and does so. Buffy sacrifices her life to save humanity.

Discussion Questions

1. Explain how Buffy illustrates Campbell's idea of destiny calling a hero.

2. Describe how Buffy takes the steps in the hero's journey as outlined by Campbell.

3. Describe how the last scene in the episode illustrates Campbell's idea of crossing the threshold and the belly of the whale.

4. Explain how *Buffy the Vampire Slayer* shows Melanie Klein's ideas about "inappropriate mothering."

4. *Clash of the Titans* (1981)

Film Data

Year: 1981

Director: Desmond Davis

Length: 118 minutes

Rated: PG

Characters/Actors

Zeus: Laurence Olivier

Hera: Claire Bloom

Thetis: Maggie Smith

Perseus: Harry Hamlin

Andromeda: Judi Bowker

Ammon: Burgess Meredith

Cassiopeia: Siân Phillips

Calibos :   Neil McCarthy

Connection to Chapters

Chapter 1. What Is Myth?

Chapter 3. Greece: Hesiod

Chapter 4. Rome: Ovid

Chapter 32. Greece: Heracles and Dionysus

Recommended Scenes

The scene of Hera and Thetis discussing Zeus' womanizing occurs at 00:21:00.

The scene of Zeus and Thetis manipulating the clay models of humans occurs at 00:13:00 through 00:16:00.

The scene of Hera deeming a human death unimportant occurs at 00:05:00.

The scenes of Zeus and Perseus discussing destiny occur at 00:25:00 and 00:34:00.

The scene of Thetis asking Zeus to forgive her son Calibos occurs at 00:14:00.

The scene of Perseus battling Medusa occurs at 01:28:00.

Viewing Information

Clash of the Titans (1981) is the last feature film for which Ray Harryhausen created the special effects. Harryhausen used stop motion animation for Medusa, the full shots of Calibos, and many of the creatures in the film.. While *Clash of the Titans* (1981) combines characters from Greek mythology with characters made up for the film, it provides a good starting point for examining the relationship between the gods and mortals.

Synopsis

The film begins with Zeus (Olivier) protecting the infant Perseus and his mother. At the same time, Zeus punishes Calibos (McCarthy) for squandering his life by transforming him into a shunned and deformed creature doomed to live in the swamp. Zeus uses wooden figures that represent humans and moves them as he wills. Thetis (Smith) is angry that Zeus will not protect her son Calibos the way Zeus protected his own child Perseus. Thetis, also angry that her son will no longer be able to marry Andromeda (Bowker), decrees that no man shall have her. Perseus (Hamlin) grows to a strong young man and meets wise Ammon (Meredith). Ammon tells him that no man may marry Andromeda until they answer her riddle. Zeus provides Perseus with a sword, shield, and helmet that render him invisible. Perseus answers the riddle and injures Calibos in fight. As Perseus and Andromeda prepare to wed, Andromeda's mother Cassiopeia (Phillips) angers Thetis by comparing her daughter's beauty to that of Thetis. Thetis decrees that Andromeda must be sacrificed as a virgin to the Kraken. Peruses goes on a quest to defeat the Kraken. He kills Calibos, cuts off Medusa's head and uses it to destroy the Kraken. Perseus and Andromeda wed. The film ends with Zeus decreeing that Peruses should be rewarded with a happy life with Andromeda. Zeus commands that Perseus, Andromeda, and Cassiopeia will be set upon the stars and constellations to perpetuate the story of Perseus's courage.

Discussion Questions

1. **Explain how the film shows Zeus to be a womanizer.**

2. **Describe how the film portrays the relationship between gods and humans.**

3. **Describe how the film portrays the relationship between the gods and their children.**

5. Clash of the Titans (2010)

Film Data

Year: 2010

Director: Louis Leterrier

Length: 106 minutes

Rated: PG-13

Characters/Actors

Perseus: Sam Worthington

Zeus: Liam Neeson

Hades: Ralph Fiennes

Calibos/Acrisius: Jason Flemyng

Io: Gemma Arterton

Andromeda: Alexa Davalos

Cassiopeia: Polly Walker

Draco: Mads Mikkelsen

Connection to Chapters

Chapter 3. Greece: Hesiod

Chapter 32. Greece: Heracles and Dionysus

Recommended Scenes

The scene of Perseus' adopted father railing against the gods occurs at 00:06:00.

The scene of Zeus expressing his anger at humans occurs at 00:10:00.

The scene of the King and Queen of Argos proclaiming a new era of man occurs at 00:16:00 through 00:19:00.

The scene of Io telling Perseus the story of his birth occurs at 00:24:00 through 00:27:00.

The scene of Perseus and his men talking about the gods occurs at 00:53:00 through 00:55:00.

The scene of Zeus and Hades arguing about man occurs at 01:26:00.

The scene of Zeus discussing Hades and man's fate with Perseus occurs at 01:34:00.

Viewing Information

Clash of the Titans (2010) is a remake of the 1981 film. The film emphasizes the role of free will and the adversarial nature of the relationship between the gods and man. *Clash of the Titans* (2010) should provide a good way to discuss the complexities of the relationship between the gods and man, the role of fate, and the ancient Greeks' view of free will.

Synopsis

King Acrisius (Flemyng) is angry at the gods for their poor treatment of humans. But Zeus (Neeson) loves man too much to punish them with destruction. Instead, Zeus makes an example of Acrisius by disguising himself as king and impregnating the queen. When the real king discovers this, he orders his wife and the infant Perseus executed. They are cast into the sea and Perseus's mother perishes, but Perseus survives. Perseus is adopted by the loving fisherman who finds him. Perseus's adopted father rails against the gods for the poor conditions present in human life. Zeus is again angry at humans for their disloyalty. Hades (Fiennes), brother of Zeus, encourages Zeus to let him lose on humanity so that humans will again worship the gods. Meanwhile, Perseus (Worthington) grows to be a strong man who is angry at the gods for killing his adopted parents. He joins an army in Argos, where Queen Cassiopeia (Walker) angers the gods. Hades swoops into Argos and tells them he will unleash the Kraken to destroy them all, unless Andromeda (Davalos) is sacrificed. However, Hades is plotting with Acrisius, who has become the monster Calibos, against Zeus. Perseus meets Io (Arterton), who tells him the story of his heritage. Perseus begins a journey to defeat the Kraken. Peruses repeatedly stated that he wishes to be a man, not a god, and initially refuses help from Zeus. Peruses eventually accepts a sword and Pegasus from Zeus, and leads men into battle to destroy the Kraken. He battles Calicos and finally kills him, visits the witches, and takes his men to the underworld to obtain the head of Medusa. Zeus visits Perseus again and offers him a home as a god in Olympus. Peruses still prefers being a man. Perseus uses the head of Medusa to defeat the Kraken and then sends Hades back to the underworld. The film ends with Zeus praising Perseus.

1. Explain how the film portrays the attitude of humans toward the gods.

2. Explain how the film portrays the attitude of the gods toward humans.

3. Describe how the film portrays the relationship between the god Zeus and his human son Perseus.

4. Describe how the film shows the role of fate and free will.

6. *The Fisher King*

Film Data

Year: 1991

Director: Terry Gilliam

Length: 137 minutes

Rated: R

Characters/Actors

Jeff Bridges: Jack

Mercedes Ruehl: Anne

Robin Williams: Parry

Amanda Plummer: Lydia

Michael Jeter: Homeless Cabaret Singer

Connection to Chapters

Part III. Heroes and Tricksters: Introductory Overview

Chapter 15. Theory: Joseph Campbell, *The Hero with a Thousand Faces* (Dave Whomsley)

Chapter 42. *Harry Potter*: A Rankian Analysis of the Hero of Hogwarts

Recommended Scenes

The scene of Parry rescuing Jack occurs at 00:17:42 through 00:21:01.

The scene of Parry telling Jack that Jack is the chosen one occurs at 00:23:55 through 00:28:16.

The scene of Jack learning Parry's true identity occurs at 00:35:17 through 00:36:20.

The scene of Parry telling Jack the story of the Fisher King occurs at 01:00:28 through 01:02:55.

The scene of Jack and Anne's double date with Lydia and Parry and Parry's attack and comatose state occurs at 01:27:22 through 01:42:00.

The scene of Jack retrieving the "Holy Grail" and Parry recovering occurs at 01:59:55 through 02:10:11.

Viewing Information

The Fisher King features outstanding performances by lead actors Jeff Bridges and Robin Williams, as well as Mercedes Ruehl, who won an Academy Award for her performance as Anne. The film deals with contemporary issues such as the power of the media and gun violence. *The Fisher King* will provide a good way to discuss Campbell's ideas about heroes, the use of myth in modern films, and the themes of heroes and rebirth.

Synopsis

Jack (Bridges), a successful radio shock-jock, is self involved and callous. He is seems headed for television success when some ill-advised words to a caller to the show change his life. The caller shoots and kills patrons in an upscale bar, and then shoots himself. The film then jumps to Jack's life three years later. Jack lives above a video store owned by his girlfriend Anne (Ruehl). He drinks heavily and is depressed. While wandering drunk, a gang of boys mistakes Jack for a homeless drunk and tries to set him on fire. Jack is saved by a group of homeless men dressed as knights, led by Parry (Williams). Parry believes he is a knight on a quest to find the Holy Grail, and that Jack has been sent to help him. When Jack learns that Parry became insane after Parry's wife was shot and killed in the upscale bar shooting, Jack feels obligated to help Parry. Jack and Anne help Parry woo Lydia (Plummer), the girl Parry loves from afar. Jack feels so good about helping Parry that he tries to return to his career and leaves his girlfriend. Just when things are looking better for Parry, Parry is beaten up and slips into a catatonic state. Doctors believe he is reexperiencing his original trauma. Jack visits Parry, but it appears Jack has returned to his old life and former self, when his conscience is reawakened. Jack steals the cup Parry believes is the Holy Grail from an Upper East Side apartment and gives it to Parry. Parry comes out of the catatonic state and resumes his romance with Lydia. Jack admits he loves Anne and they reconcile. Both men are better for the experience of knowing each other and the film ends with Jack and Parry in Central Park.

1. **Explain how both Jack and Parry take some of the steps in the hero's journey as outlined by Campbell.**

2. **Describe how the film shows Jack experiencing a rebirth.**

3. **Describe how the film shows the importance of hero myths to the characters.**

7. Harry Potter and the Sorcerer's Stone

Film Data

Year: 2001

Director: Chris Columbus

Length: 152 minutes

Rated: PG

Characters/Actors

Richard Harris:	Professor Albus Dumbledore
Maggie Smith:	Professor Minerva McGonagall
Robbie Coltrane:	Rubeus Hagrid
Daniel Radcliffe:	Harry Potter
Rupert Grint:	Ron Weasley
Emma Watson:	Hermione Granger
Richard Bremmer:	He Who Must Not Be Named
Fiona Shaw:	Aunt Petunia Dursley
Harry Melling:	Dudley Dursley
Geraldine Somerville:	Lily Potter

Connection to Chapters

Chapter 42. *Harry Potter:* A Rankian Analysis of the Hero of Hogwarts

Recommended Scenes

The scene in the wand shop occurs at 00:25:21 through 00:28:38.

The scene of Hermione telling Harry his parents were seekers occurs at 01:27:00. The scene of the Quidditch match occurs at 01:20:14 through 01:23:09.

The scene of Harry seeing his parents in the mirror occurs at 01:32:54 through 01:36:12.

The scene of the battle with He Who Must Not Be Named (Voldemort) occurs at 02:08:43 through 02:13:57.

The scene of Dumbledore explaining what happened to Harry occurs at 02:15:00 through 02:16:51.

The scene of Hagrid saying goodbye to Harry occurs at 02:21:50 through the end of the film.

Viewing Information

The film provides an excellent companion to the material discussed by Grimes. *Harry Potter and the Sorcerer's Stone* contains rich examples of positive and negative mother and father figures. The film should provide a very enjoyable way to discuss Grimes' theories about using Rank's analysis for Harry Potter.

Synopsis

Harry Potter (Radcliffe) lives with his mean aunt, uncle, and cousin. On his eleventh birthday, Rubeus Hagrid (Coltrane) tells him that he is really a wizard and his parents were killed by the evil He Who Must Not Be Named (Bremmer). Hagrid takes Harry to Hogwarts to learn magic. Along the way, Harry befriends fellow students Ron Weasley (Grint) and Hermione Granger (Watson). The three friends study potions, play Quidditch, and explore their magical surroundings. They learn that someone is trying to steal the sorcerer's stone, which can grant immortality. The three friends have several adventures, culminating in an encounter with a three-headed dog followed by a dangerous game of chess. After Ron is injured, Harry alone must face He Who Must Not Be Named. Harry retrieves the stone, and the evil one is defeated for the time being. The film ends with Harry and his friends successfully completing their first year at Hogwarts. The students go home for the summer, but Harry knows that Hogwarts is his real home.

Discussion Questions

1. **Describe how the film illustrates Grimes' ideas about positive father figures.**

2. Describe how the film illustrates Grimes' ideas about negative father figures.

3. Explain how the film shows Grimes' updating of Rank's ideas regarding mother figures.

8. Hercules

Film Data

Year: 1959

Director: Pietro Francisci

Length: 107 minutes

Rated: PG

Characters/Actors

Hercules: Steve Reeves

Iole: Sylva Koscina

Jason: Fabrizio Mioni

Pelias: Ivo Garrani

Antea, Queen of the Amazons: Gianna Maria Canale

Connection to Chapters

Chapter 32. Greece: Heracles and Dionysus

Recommended Scenes

The scene of Hercules training the young men of Iolcus occurs at 00:19:40.

The scene of Hercules discussing his destiny with the oracle occurs at 00:35:32.

The scene of Iole and Hercules discussing their new destinies occurs at 00:49:11.

The scene of Jason discussing his father's wishes and his conscience with Hercules occurs at 01:29:55.

Viewing Information

Hercules is the dubbed version of the 1958 Italian film *Le fatiche di Ercole*. Even American bodybuilder Steve Reeves is dubbed. Although the plot is somewhat convoluted and the film at times is unintentionally comical, the character of Hercules remains compelling. While *Hercules* combines characters and events from several stories, the film does refer to three of the labors of Hercules. The film's view of Hercules as a monogamous and moral individual who wishes to live a traditional mortal life provides a good starting point for examining the many facets of the character of Hercules.

Synopsis

Hercules (Reeves) arrives in Iolcus after saving the life of Iole (Koscina), the scantily clad daughter of King Pelias (Garrani). He is viewed with suspicion by the king, but is hailed as hero by the young men in the kingdom, and they attempt to emulate his strength and prowess. Hercules and Iole fall in love, but their romance is soon interrupted. Hercules kills a deadly lion, defeats the Cretan bull and helps Jason (Mioni) reclaim his throne from evil King Pelias. Along the way, Hercules proclaims his desire to live as a mortal and have a family. After Jason and his men succumb to the charms of Antea, Queen of the Amazons (Canale), and her Amazonian women, Hercules rescues them and returns with Jason to Iolcus. Jason takes his rightful places as king, and Hercules and Iole embrace.

Discussion Questions

1. **Explain how the film shows Hercules to be more than just a powerful and savage warrior.**

2. **Describe how Hercules is a role model for young men.**

3. **Describe how the film portrays Hercules' sexuality.**

4. **What role do destiny and free will play in the lives of the characters?**

9. *Hercules* (animated)

Film Data

Year: 1997

Director: Ron Clements and John Musker

Length: 93 minutes

Rated: G

Characters/Actors

Tate Donovan: Hercules (voice)

Josh Keaton: Young Hercules (singing voice)

Danny DeVito: Philoctetes (voice)

James Woods: Hades; Lord of the Underworld (voice)

Rip Torn: Zeus (voice)

Samantha Eggar: Hera, Hercules' Mother (voice)

Susan Egan: Meg (voice)

Connection to Chapters

Chapter 15. Theory: Joseph Campbell, *The Hero with a Thousand Faces* (Dave Whomsley)

Chapter 32. Greece: Heracles and Dionysus

Recommended Scenes

The scene of the witches making a prediction for Hades occurs at 00:09:20.

The scene of Zeus and Hercules being reunited occurs at 00:21:35.

The scene of the gospel song about Hercules' adventures as a hero occurs at 00:48:53.

The scene of the reference to Hercules' labors occurs at 00:54:49 through 00:55:39.

The scene of Hercules and Hades making the deal for Meg's life occurs at 1:08:35.

The scene of Hercules offering to trade his life for Meg's life and rescuing Meg from the underworld occurs at 1:21:00.

The scene of Hercules returning to Zeus and Hera with Meg and resolving his adventure occurs at 1:23:57.

Viewing Information

Hercules is an animated Disney musical with gospel-style music by frequent Disney composer Alan Menken and lyrics by David Zippel. The film tells a story that features some of the characters in the Heracles myth. Although many details have been changed to make the story appropriate for children, the film contains sly references and humor that adults will appreciate. While the film does not deal directly with the labors of Heracles, *Hercules* should be an enjoyable way to introduce the material about Heracles. The film is also a good way to illustrate the many ways Joseph Campbell's ideas about heroes are found in old myths and contemporary retellings.

Synopsis

Hercules (Donovan) is the beloved son of Zeus (Torn) and Hera (Eggar). The three witches tell the evil Hades (Woods) to release the titans in eighteen years. They predict that Zeus will fall and Hades will be victorious, but if Hercules fights, Hades will fall. Hades sends a potion to harm Hercules. Hercules is made mortal and is adopted by a childless couple. However, because Hercules did not drink the last drop of the potion, he retains his strength. Hercules grows up and meets his true parents. Zeus tell Hercules that he cannot return to Olympus until he proves that he is a true hero. Philoctetes (DeVito) trains Hercules to be a hero. Hercules performs many brave deeds, including rescuing the lovely Meg (Eggar). But Meg is working for Hades to discover Hercules' weakness. Meg and Hercules fall in love and she eventually helps Hercules. Meg gets hurt, her agreement with Hades is invalidated ,and Hercules becomes a god. Hades traps Meg in the underworld, and Hercules offers to trade his life for Meg's. Hercules survives the underworld because he is a god, and rescues Meg. Hercules and Zeus return to Olympus. Zeus proclaims that Hercules is a true hero because he was willing to sacrifice his life for Meg's. Hercules chooses to stay with Meg and remain mortal. They kiss and live happily on earth.

Discussion Questions

1. Explain how the film portrays Hercules' many-sided personality.

2. Describe how the film portrays the power and personality of the gods and the relationship between the gods and humans.

3. Describe how the film shows Hercules following the steps of Campbell's hero's journey.

10. I Am Legend

Film Data

Year: 2007

Director: Francis Lawrence

Length: 101 minutes

Rated: PG-13

Characters/Actors

Will Smith:	Robert Neville
Alice Braga:	Anna
Charlie Tahan:	Ethan

Connection to Chapters

Chapter 13. The Bible: Genesis (Flood)

Chapter 15. Theory: Joseph Campbell, *The Hero with a Thousand Faces* (Dave Whomsley)

Chapter 41. *Stagecoach* and *Firefly:* The Journey into the Unknown in Westerns and Science Fiction

Recommended Scenes

The scene of Neville getting his family out of New York occurs at 00:13:04 through 00:15:11.

The scene of Neville and Sam being attacked by zombies and Neville experimenting on a zombie occurs at 00:31:20 through 00:37:40.

The scene of Neville first talking to Anna about the virus occurs at 01:05:54 through 01:13:47.

The scene of Neville discussing Bob Marley with Anna and Anna discussing God's plan occurs at 01:16:16 through 01:20:13.

The scene of the final battle with the zombies and the resolution of the story occurs at 01:26:36 through the end of the film.

Viewing Information

I Am Legend is based on the 1954 novel written by Richard Matheson. The film features a strong performance by Will Smith, and most of the film consists of Smith's character talking to his dog and himself. The film should be an effective and enjoyable way to begin discussing destruction myths. *I Am Legend* also provides a good example of some of the steps of a hero's journey as described Joseph Campbell. This film should also be a good way to explore the way this contemporary futuristic film reflects the concerns of its audience.

Synopsis

Robert Neville (Smith) seems to be the only person left in New York City. Flashback scenes reveal that three years after a cure for cancer was found, a byproduct of the cure caused a deadly virus. Most of those infected die, and the others become vicious killers who look and act like zombies. Only a small percentage of the population is immune. Neville is immune. He was an army colonel and scientist who worked on the cure. He tried to help his wife and children escape a quarantined Manhattan, but his family was killed. Now he spends his days working on a cure for the virus, looking for other human survivors and walking with his dog Sam. The zombie creatures cannot stand light, but roam the streets when the sun goes down. Neville spends his nights in his locked house. He meets Anna (Braga), a young woman traveling with a young boy Ethan (Tahan), after they save Neville's life. Anna tells him about a colony of survivors in Vermont. At first, Neville does not believe her. After the creatures break into the house, Neville, Anna, and Ethan hide in Neville's lab. While there, Anna notices that a zombie test subject shows signs of returning to her human form. Neville gives Anna the subject's blood containing the cure for the virus and tells her to take it to Vermont. Neville stays in the lab and uses a grenade to kill the zombies and kills himself. The film ends with Anna reaching the colony with the cure and seeing other humans. She explains that Neville gave his life to save humanity.

Discussion Questions

1. **Explain how the film reflects the concerns of its audience.**

2. **Describe how Robert Neville takes some of the steps in the hero's journey as outlined by Campbell.**

3. **Explain the way the film is similar to the biblical flood story.**

11. Into the Woods

Film Data

Year: 1991

Director: James Lapine

Length: 153 minutes

Rated: N/A

Characters/Actors

Bernadette Peters:	The Witch
Chip Zien:	Baker
Joanna Gleason:	Baker's wife
Tom Aldredge:	Narrator/Mysterious Man
Robert Westenberg:	Wolf/Cinderella's Prince
Kim Crosby:	Cinderella
Danielle Ferland:	Little Red Riding Hood
Ben Wright:	Jack
Barbara Bryne:	Jack's mother
Pamela Winslow:	Rapunzel

Connection to Chapters

Chapter 34. Applying Theory: How to Perform a Jungian Analysis

Chapter 37. Germany: Grimms' *Household Tales*

Recommended Scenes

The scene of the Witch telling the Baker how to reverse the curse occurs at 00:12:20.

The scene of Little Red Riding Hood and the wolf occurs at 00:18:24 through 00:21:12.

The scene of the Baker and his wife debating the morality of cheating Jack occurs at 00:25:02 through 00:26:05.

The scene of the princes singing about their dissatisfaction with marriage occurs at 01:34:31.

The scene of the Baker's wife and Cinderella's Prince having a tryst and then discussing it occurs at 01:48:42 through 01:56:12.

The scene of Little Red Riding Hood expressing reservations about killing the giant and Cinderella, the Baker, and Jack singing about the ambiguities of life of occurs at 02:15:35 through 02:20:23.

The scene of the resolution of the story occurs at 02:22:21 through the end of the film.

Viewing Information

Into the Woods is a filmed version of the Tony Award-winning Broadway musical. Stephen Sondheim wrote the music and lyrics. The book was written by James Lapine, and was inspired by Bruno Bettelheim's *Uses of Enchantment.* The musical's first act combines characters from the Grimms' tales and unifies their stories. The second act imagines what happens after fairy tales end. This is a musical for adults, featuring serious themes and much humor. This excellent musical should provide an enjoyable way to examine the household tales and their relevance for adult audiences.

Synopsis

Into the Woods follows familiar fairy tale characters Cinderella (Crosby) Jack (Wright), Little Red Riding Hood (Ferland) and others. Three characters invented for *Into the Woods,* the Baker (Zien) and his wife (Gleason) and an evil Witch (Peters), help tie the various other story lines together. A narrator (Aldredge) recounts and comments on the story. In Act I, the audience learns that the Baker and his wife want to have a child. They live next door to an evil witch who tells them that when the Baker was a boy, his father stole some beans from the witch's garden for the Baker's pregnant mother. The witch took the Baker's sibling and placed a curse on the Baker, making him unable to have children. The witch tells the Baker and his wife that she will reverse this curse and allow them to have a baby if they bring her certain items. The search for these items take the couple on a journey that intersects with Little Red Riding Hood and her encounter with the Wolf (Westenberg), Jack and his adventures with a giant and a beanstalk, and Cinderella and her Prince (Westenberg). When Act I ends, the Baker's wife is pregnant, the witch is no longer a witch, and all of the other characters' problems are resolved happily. Act II imagines what might occur after the happy endings. A giant attacks the town, and the characters must work together to destroy it. Along the way, the characters examine what they really desire from life. Cinderella's Prince is unfaithful, the Baker's wife is killed by the giant, and other characters suffer losses. The group kills the giant together. Cinderella and the Baker raise his baby together, and they agree to take care of Jack and Little Red Riding Hood.

Discussion Questions

1. **Explain how the film reflects contemporary values.**

2. **Explain how the film is consistent with the Grimms' ideas of characters developing the moral values of charity and self-sacrifice.**

3. **Describe the ways that the film, like the stories of the Grimm Brothers, is directed primarily at adults.**

12. *Joseph Campbell and the Power of Myth,* Episode 1: "The Hero's Adventure"

Film Data

Year: 1988

Executive Producer: Joan Konner and Alvin H. Perlmutter

Length: 60 minutes

Rated: N/A (television mini-series)

Characters/Actors

Joseph Campbell: Himself

George Lucas: Himself

Bill Moyers: Himself/Interviewer

Connection to Chapters

Chapter 15. Theory: Joseph Campbell, *The Hero with a Thousand Faces* (Dave Whomsley)

Recommended Scenes

The scene of Bill Moyers introducing Joseph Campbell and the documentary occurs at 00:02:55 through 00:04:21.

The scene of Campbell discussing religious figures occurs at 00:11:54 through 00:14:55.

The scene of Campbell discussing *Star Wars* occurs at 00:17:17 through 00:24:01.

The scene of Campbell discussing the individual as a hero occurs at 00:27:00.

The scene of Campbell telling the Iroquois tale occurs at 00:28:42 through 00:34:14.

The scene of Campbell discussing dragons and inner desires occurs at 00:36:00 through 00:41:10.

Joseph Campbell and the Power of Myth is a six-part documentary television mini-series. It consists of interviews of acclaimed scholar Joseph Campbell by Bill Moyers. The interviews were conducted in 1987 shortly before Campbell's death. A recommended special feature is a fifteen-minute segment of selections from the 2000 documentary *The Mythology of "Star Wars."* In these selections Bill Moyers interviews *Star Wars* writer/director George Lucas. Episode 1, "The Hero's Adventure," is an excellent way to discuss Campbell's ideas about heroes.

Synopsis

Bill Moyers provides a brief introduction to Joseph Campbell and the series at the start of episode one. In episode 1, "The Hero's Adventure," Campbell discusses the motifs of the hero's adventures in many different cultures. Campbell talks about the religion and the hero's journey exemplified by Moses, Jesus, Buddha, and Mohammed. Moyers and Campbell also devote time to a discussion of the hero cycle in the film *Star Wars*, and they show and discuss specific clips from the film. Toward the end of this episode, Campbell relates the hero to present-day individuals. He uses the example of an Iroquois myth. Campbell and Moyers conclude by discussing the various cultural and psychological meaning of dragons, and the relevance of this for people today.

Discussion Questions

1. **Explain how Campbell uses religious figures to illustrate the hero's journey in the episode.**

2. **Describe how Campbell and Moyers use the film *Star Wars* to discuss the hero's journey in the episode.**

3. **Describe how Campbell contends in the episode that we are all heroes in our own lives.**

13. The Matrix

Film Data

Year: 1999

Director: The Wachowski Brothers

Length: 136 minutes

Rated: R

Characters/Actors

Keanu Reeves:	Neo
Laurence Fishburne:	Morpheus
Carrie-Anne Moss:	Trinity
Hugo Weaving:	Agent Smith
Gloria Foster:	Oracle
Joe Pantoliano:	Cypher

Connection to Chapters

Part IIA. Myths of Creation and Destruction–Creation: Introductory Overview

Chapter 5. The Bible: Genesis (Creation)

Chapter 15. Theory: Joseph Campbell, *The Hero with a Thousand Faces* (Dave Whomsley)

Chapter 33. Theory: C. G. Jung, *Man and His Symbols*

Recommended Scenes

The scene of Neo's first encounter with Agent Smith occurs at 00:17:09 through 00:21:50.

The scene of Morpheus offering Neo the choice of the red or blue pill and then freeing Neo occurs at 00:25:47 through 00:134:59.

The scene of Morpheus explaining the history of the matrix occurs at 00:41:28 through 00:46:29.

The scene of Neo visiting the oracle occurs at 01:14:30.

The scene of Neo rescuing Morpheus occurs at 01:41:06.

The scene of occurs Neo finally defeating Agent Smith occurs at 02:00:40 through 02:06:59.

Viewing Information

The Matrix is a science fiction action film. It was the first of a series of *Matrix* films. *The Matrix* will provide an excellent catalyst for class discussion about Joseph Campbell's hero quest as well as many of C. J. Jung's idea. The film is also a good way to introduce the topic of creation myths.

Synopsis

Computer programmer and hacker Thomas/Neo (Reeves) has questions about his world. The legendary Morpheus (Fishburne) contacts Neo to arrange a meeting. After narrowly escaping police questioning, Trinity (Moss) and her crew bring Neo to Morpheus. Neo learns that the world as he knows it is a computer-generated program called the matrix. Artificial intelligence has created a dream world to control humans so the machines can use the body heat of humans as batteries. Humans are grown, not born, and they live in a dream state. Humans are connected by wires to machines. A small band of rebels lives on a ship in the real world. Morpheus believes a prophecy that says Neo is the one destined to save humanity from the matrix. Morpheus trains Neo, and Neo shows that he is the chosen one. The rebels are betrayed by fellow crew member Cypher (Pantoliano), and some of them are killed. Neo and Trinity fall in love. Neo is able to defeat his nemesis Agent Smith (Weaving) and other enemies inside the matrix. By the end of the film, Neo has embraced his destiny and returns to the matrix to continue his fight to free humanity.

Discussion Questions

1. **Describe how Neo takes the steps in the hero's journey as outlined by Campbell.**

2. **Explain how the story told by the film is a creation myth.**

3. **Explain how the film refers to the ideas of C. J. Jung.**

14. *Mighty Aphrodite*

Film Data

Year: 1995

Director: Woody Allen

Length: 95 minutes

Rated: R

Characters/Actors

Lenny:	Woody Allen
Leader:	F. Murray Abraham
Amanda:	Helena Bonham Carter
Kevin:	Michael Rapaport
Linda Ash:	Mira Sorvino
Laius:	David Ogden Stiers
Tiresias:	Jack Warden
Jocasta:	Olympia Dukakis

Connection to Chapters

Chapter 21. Greece: Sophocles' *Oedipus the King*

Chapter 22. Theory: Claude Lévi-Strauss, *The Structural Study of Myth*

Recommended Scenes

The scene of the Leader refusing to help Lenny in his search occurs at 00:21:40.

The scene of the Greek Chorus warning Lenny about searching for his son's mother occurs at 00:18:12.

The scene of Jocasta, Laius, and the Greek Chorus talking about Oedipus occurs from 00:05:36 through 00:07:00.

The scene of the Greek Chorus talking about irony occurs at 01:28:00.

Viewing Information

Mighty Aphrodite is a comedy written by, directed by, and starring Woody Allen. The film tells the story of a modern New York couple who adopt a child and is interspersed with a Greek Chorus led by Leader (Abraham). The Greek Chorus uses characters from and speaks in the style of *Oedipus the King.* The Greek Chorus also mixes contemporary language and expression with some of the ideas in *Oedipus the King.* The film provides an enjoyable and informative way to begin an examination of Oedipus, and provides a good start for a discussion of the role of the Greek Chorus and the concept of irony.

Synopsis

New York sportswriter Lenny (Allen) and his ambitious wife Amanda (Carter) adopt a son and name him Max. The couple soon experiences marital problems, but Lenny loves his smart and funny son. Lenny becomes obsessed with finding his son's biological mother. Throughout this film, a Greek Chorus, using some of the characters from *Oedipus,* narrates and comments on the story. Members of the Greek Chorus also interact with and advise Lenny. Lenny learns that his son's biological mother is Linda Ash (Sorvino), a porn star and prostitute who wishes to be an actress. He contacts Linda against the advice of the Chorus, and they become friends. Lenny helps Linda leave the prostitution business and introduces her to handsome boxer Kevin (Rapaport). Kevin and Linda date, but Kevin breaks off the relationship when he learns about Linda's past. Meanwhile, Tiresias (Warden) appears as a blind beggar and tells Lenny that his wife Amanda is having an affair. Lenny and Linda console each other by sleeping together. Lenny and Amanda realize they still love each other and reconcile. Linda leaves town and marries a pilot and has a child. The Greek Chorus tells us the child is Lenny's. Near the end of the film, Lenny, Linda and their children run into each other in a department store. Both Lenny and Linda are happy with their lives, and unaware that the other has their child. The film ends with the Leader of the Greek Chorus commenting on the irony of the situation, followed by a song and dance by the Greek Chorus.

Discussion Questions

1. Explain the function of the Greek Chorus in the film.

2. Describe how the film refers to Freud's use of *Oedipus.*

3. Describe how the film shows the overvaluing of blood relations.

4. Describe how irony is used in the film.

15. Oedipus Rex

Film Data

Year: 1967

Director: Pier Paolo Pasolini

Length: 104 minutes

Rated: N/A

Characters/Actors

Jocasta: Silvana Mangano

Oedipus: Franco Citti

Merope: Alida Valli

Creon: Carmelo Bene

Tiresias: Julian Beck

Laius: Luciano Bartoli

Connection to Chapters

Chapter 21. Greece: Sophocles, *Oedipus the King*

Chapter 22. Theory: Claude Lévi-Strauss, *The Structural Study of Myth*

Recommended Scenes

The scene in Fascist Italy occurs from the start of the film through 00:11:57.

The scene of Oedipus cheating at his discus match occurs at 00:18:01.

The scene of the laughing oracle telling Oedipus his fate occurs at 00:35:32.

The scene of Oedipus fighting and killing Laius and his men occurs from 00:35:25 through 00:43:41.

The scene of Oedipus talking to and killing the sphinx occurs from 00:49:22 through 00:50:38.

The scene of Oedipus and Jocasta sleeping together for the first time occurs at 00:54:32.

The scene of Tiresias telling Oedipus the truth occurs from 01:08:13 through 01:14:31.

The scene of Oedipus and Jocasta discussing the truth occurs from 01:25:34 through 01:28:59.

The scene of Oedipus discovering Jocasta dead and blinding himself occurs at 01:36:14.

Viewing Information

Oedipus Rex is written and directed by acclaimed filmmaker Pier Paolo Pasolini, and is based on the play by Sophocles. There are modern scenes of Fascist Italy at the start of the film and scenes of then-contemporary Italy at the end of the film. The bulk of the film in between tells a version of *Oedipus Rex*. This section of *Oedipus Rex* was filmed in Morocco. The film is a good companion piece to the play by Sophocles, and comparison and contrast of the two works should start an engaging discussion about the themes of the play. The film's use of visual techniques and the modern sections of the film should make a fine starting point for a discussion of Freud's ideas inspired by this myth.

Synopsis

Oedipus Rex begins with a short segment in twentieth-century Fascist Italy. A mother cares for her newborn son while the baby's father, a soldier in uniform, feels jealous of his son. The scene then shifts to a barren desert, where a man leaves an infant on the ground. A shepherd finds the baby and gives him to a childless king and queen. Oedipus (Citti) grows up and is haunted by bad dreams. He visits the oracle to ask their meaning. The oracle laughs at Oedipus and reveals that his fate is to kill his father and make love with his mother. In an attempt to escape his fate, Oedipus wanders the desert toward Thebes. He encounters a group of men who order him to leave the road. Chases and fights ensue, and Oedipus kills all but one of them. Oedipus then kills the sphinx, thought to be the cause of the troubles plaguing Thebes. Oedipus is rewarded with marriage to Queen Jocasta (Mangano) and becomes King. After this, the title "Part Two" appears on the screen. This section of the film opens with a crying baby in the desert, surrounded by corpses. King Oedipus is asked to find the cause of a terrible plague afflicting Thebes. Oedipus searches for the man who murdered the former King, Laius (Bartoli). Blind Tiresias (Beck) tells Oedipus the truth. Oedipus does not want to believe that he has killed his father, married his mother, and caused the plague. Jocasta realizes the truth and hangs herself. Oedipus sees Jocasta dead and pokes out his eyes. He wanders blind, playing a flute. The film ends with blind Oedipus playing a flute in present-day Italy. Oedipus is led through the city to a meadow where the infants in the film were held. Oedipus proclaims, "Life ends where it begins."

Discussion Questions

1. **Describe the film's view of fate and free will in the life of Oedipus.**

2. **Describe how the film refers to Freud's theories about *Oedipus*.**

3. **Explain how the film differs in significant ways from the play *Oedipus the King*.**

16. Opera Jawa (Requiem from Java)

Film Data

Year: 2006

Director: Garin Nugroho

Length: 120 minutes

Rated: N/A

Characters/Actors

Martinus Miroto: Setio

Eko Supriyanto: Ludiro

Artika Sari Devi: Siti

Retno Maruti: Sukesi

Jecko Siompo Pui: Anom

Connection to Chapters

Chapter 18. India: The *Ramayana*

Recommended Scenes

The scene of Seito singing to Siti about faithfulness occurs at 00:44:32.

The scene of Ludiro's mother extolling Siti's goodness occurs at 00:20:13 through 00:21:23.

The scene of Seito rejecting Siti occurs at 00:33:43.

The scene of Siti and Ludiro dancing on Ludiro's bed occurs at 00:44:12 through 00:47:30.

The scene of Siti again going to Ludiro occurs at 01:08:19 through 01:15:59.

The scene of the dancers singing about Sinta and Ram occurs at 01:29:29.

The scene of Seito killing Siti occurs at 01:41:59.

The film begins with a text stating that it is a version of the abduction of Sita (referred to in this film as Sinta), often dramatized by Javanese dance and puppetry. This contemporary retelling imagines that both men love Sinta, and focuses on Sinta's conflict and purity. The film is in Indonesian with English subtitles, but almost all of the words are sung, and much of the story is told through movement, so you should not be daunted by the subtitles. *Opera Jawa* is an excellent way to discuss the *Ramayana* and its cultural importance today.

Synopsis

Siti (Devi) and her husband Setio (Miroto) appear happy and in love. Siti used to dance the role of Sinta, but now Siti and Sieto farm and make pottery, and they struggle to get by. Ludiro (Supriyanto), a wealthy butcher, also loves Siti and pursues her while her husband is away selling his wares. Siti is nostalgic for her life as a dancer and is tempted by the wealthy and exciting Ludiro. She feels guilty about her fantasies, and bemoans her inability to tell right from wrong. Siti and Ludiro participate in a group dance. When Sieto returns from his trip, he seems suspicious and rejects Siti's embraces. When Setio leaves again, Siti follows a trail of candles to Ludiro's bed. In a scene involving shadows, song, and dance, Siti and Ludiro share a passionate encounter. She expresses guilt over her attraction and runs away. When Sieto returns, he finds Siti gone and wonders if love and fidelity are also gone. An anguished Seito uses clay and puppets in a bizarre performance ritual to express his feelings. While this is happening, the economic conditions in the village worsen, and protesters demonstrate against poverty and their exploitation by the rich. There are news reports of escalating violence. Unable to forget Siti, Ludiro lures her to him with a long red dance scarf. Siti goes to Ludiro, but again returns to her husband. However, now their relationship is damaged. Sieto joins the protesters. Ludiro is killed. Sita sings about the joys of being a woman. Siti and Seito embrace on the beach. Seito then kills Siti and tears out her heart. The film ends with a radio news station report on the arrest of Sieto for the murders of Siti and Ludiro.

Discussion Questions

1. **Describe how the characters in the film illustrate the concept of *dharma*.**

2. **Explain how the film shows the importance of the *Ramayana* in the lives of these contemporary characters.**

3. **Describe how the film incorporates ancient traditions surrounding the myth.**

17. Pan's Labyrinth (El laberinto del fauno)

Film Data

Year: 2006

Director: Guillermo del Toro

Length: 119 minutes

Rated: R

Characters/Actors

Ivana Baquero:	Ofelia
Sergi López:	Vidal
Maribel Verdú:	Mercedes
Doug Jones:	Fauno/Pale Man
Ariadna Gil:	Carmen
Álex Angulo:	Doctor

Connection to Chapters

Chapter 15. Theory: Joseph Campbell, The *Hero with a Thousand Faces* (Dave Whomsley)

Chapter 33. Theory: C.G. Jung, *Man and His Symbols*

Chapter 37. Germany: Grimms' *Household Tales*

Chapter 42. *Harry Potter*: A Rankian Analysis of the Hero of Hogwarts

Recommended Scenes

The scene of Ofelia's initial encounter with the fairy and faun occurs at 00:21:00 through 00:26:00.

The scene of Ofelia battling the toad occurs at 00:35:00 through 00:39:00.

The scene of Ofelia encountering the Pale Man and eating grapes begins at 00:54:00.

The scene of the angry faun telling Ofelia that she broke the rules occurs at 01:19:00.

The scene of the doctor disobeying Vidal and then being shot occurs at 01:25:00.

The scene of the faun giving Ofelia one last chance and the resolution of the story occurs at 01:38:10 through the end of the film,

Viewing Information

Pan's Labyrinth is the work of respected Mexican filmmaker Guillermo del Toro. The film is in Spanish with English subtitles. *Pan's Labyrinth* begins with the recitation of a fairy tale. This sets the stage for the two stories in this film. The story of Ofelia and her encounters with the faun in the labyrinth contain many elements present in the Grimm brothers' fairy tales. The second story also involves Ofelia and the aftermath of World War II. This second story is harrowing and serious, yet both stories share some common features. *Pan's Labyrinth* is an excellent example of a fairy tale directed at adults. It is visually stunning and the plot is engrossing. The film should provide an excellent way to examine the ideas of Joseph Campbell and Otto Rank about heroes and Jung's theories about the unconscious, as well as providing a good way to discuss household tales.

Synopsis

Pan's Labyrinth takes place in 1944 Spain. Cruel and vicious Captain Vidal (López) hunts the anti-Franco rebels hiding in the woods. Vidal's wife Carmen (Gil) is pregnant with their child and Carmen and Carmen's daughter Ofelia (Baquero) move to the Captain's house. Vidal treats both of them with disdain, seeming to only care for his unborn child. Ofelia has an encounter with a fairy that at first appears to be a praying mantis. The fairy takes her to a creature called a faun (Jones) who looks like a cross between a human, a goat and a large malevolent elf. The faun tells Ofelia that she is really a princess from a magical kingdom and must complete three tasks in order to return there. While Ofelia attempts to complete the tasks, life continues to grow more difficult in Vidal's house. Vidal shoots and tortures rebels and Carmen grows ill. Vidal's maid Mercedes (Verdú) befriends Ofelia, and Ofelia learns that Mercedes is secretly helping the rebels. Ofelia keeps this secret. Carmen's condition worsens and she dies after giving birth to a son. Mercedes is caught by the Captain, but escapes. The faun tells Ofelia that her last chance to return to the kingdom is to bring her brother to the labyrinth. She does so, but when she learns that a few drops of her brother's innocent blood is necessary to open the portal to the kingdom, she refuses to hurt her brother. Vidal discovers her, takes the baby, and shoots Ofelia. Carmen and the rebels take the baby to raise and kill Vidal. The film ends with Ofelia dying in the labyrinth, and then making a spiritual return to her kingdom. We are told that she ruled wisely for many centuries and was loved by her people.

Discussion Questions

1. Explain how the film illustrates the maturation and initiation cycle, as well as Rank's ideas of the family romance.

2. Describe how Ofelia takes the steps in the hero's journey as outlined by Campbell.

3. Describe the ways that the film, like the stories of the Grimm Brothers, is directed primarily at adults.

4. Describe the ways that the film refers to Jung's ideas about individuation and Rank's ideas about heroes.

18. Popol Vuh: The Creation Myth of the Maya

Film Data

Year: 1988

Director: Patricia Amlin

Length: 60 minutes

Rated: N/A

Characters/Actors

Larry George, Yakima Nation: Narrator

Hun Ah Pu: Hunter

X Balan Ke: Jaguar Deer

Connection to Chapters

Chapter 11. Mesoamerica: *Popol Vuh*

Recommended Scenes

The scene of the creators trying to make intelligent beings occurs at 00:04:45 through 00:06:22 of Part 1.

The scene of the twins talking to the rat and learning about their destiny occurs at 00:07:17 of Part 3.

The scene of the twins planting stalks of corn for their mother and grandmother occurs at 00:05:55 of Part 4.

The scenes of the twins' feats in the underworld occurs at 00:00:45 of Part 5 through 00:05:22 of Part 6.

The scenes of the death of the twins, the beggars defeating the lords of the underworld and the resolution of the story occur at 00:06:26 of Part 6 through 00:03:54 of Part 7.

Popol Vuh: The Creation Myth of the Maya is an animated film that tells the story of the *Popol Vuh*. According to a note at the beginning of the film, the drawings used for the animation are taken directly from classic Maya pottery. The film is available on YouTube (http://theinnkeeperstail.blogspot.com/search?q=popol+vuh) in seven parts. A narrator tells the story, and occasionally the characters use dialogue. The film starts with the creation of humanity and then tells the story of the birth of the Hero Twins and their adventures. The film is an enjoyable and interesting way to introduce the *Popol Vuh*.

Synopsis

Part 1 tells the story of Grandmother of Day and Light attempting to create intelligent beings to worship their creators. After creating and destroying beings of mud and wood, humans are created. Then the story of the Hero Twins, Hunter and Jaguar Deer, begins. Part 2 tells about the fathers of the twins, two brothers who were artists and magicians, as well as ball players. The brothers are invited to play ball in the underworld, but they are tricked and killed by the lords of the underworld. The rest of Part 2 recounts the story of Little Blood, a young virgin who becomes pregnant with the sons of the dead brothers. The pregnant girl defeats the lords of the underworld when they try to kill her. She climbs to earth to meet her children's grandmother, who initially doubts her story. The Hero Twins are born and grow up in Part 3. They learn their destiny is to be ballplayers like their fathers. In Part 4, the twins play ball using the equipment belonging to their fathers. Like their fathers, the twins are invited to play ball in the underworld. In Part 5, the twins arrive in the underworld and refuse to be tricked as their fathers were. They outwit the lords of the underworld and pass a series of tests. In Part 6, the twins see a vision of their own deaths. The twins arrange for a seer to tell the lords that when the twins die, the lords should chop up their bones and scatter them in the ocean. The twins then jump into a fire and are killed. Their bones are scattered. In Part 7, two beggars appear and begin doing magical feats. They are invited to the underworld. The beggars kill all of the lords in the underworld, and then reveal that they are the Hero Twins and have avenged their fathers' deaths. After the twins defeat all in the underworld forever, the twins walk into the sky and become the sun and the moon.

Discussion Questions

1. **Describe how the film portrays the view the creators had of early man.**

2. **Explain how the film portrays the significance of corn.**

3. **Describe the cultural insights provided in the film's portrayal of the achievements of the twins.**

19. Red Riding Hood

Film Data

Year: 2011

Director: Catherine Hardwicke

Length: 100 minutes

Rated: PG-13

Characters/Actors

Valerie: Amanda Seyfried

Solomon: Gary Oldman

Cesaire: Billy Burke

Peter: Shiloh Fernandez

Henry: Max Irons

Suzette: Virginia Madsen

Grandmother: Julie Christie

Connection to Chapters

Chapter 34. Applying Theory: How to Perform a Jungian Analysis

Chapter 37. Germany: Grimms' *Household Tales*

Recommended Scenes

The scene of Valerie talking about being a good girl and encountering Peter occurs at 00:4:10.

The scene of Peter and Valerie embracing before being interrupted occurs at 00:39:00 through 00:40:08.

The scene of the wolf speaking to Valerie for the first time occurs at 00:44:15.

The scene of Valerie suspecting her grandmother of being the wolf occurs at 01:19:02.

The scene of Valerie confronting her father, killing the wolf, and changing her life occurs from 01:24:20 through the end of the film.

Viewing Information

Red Riding Hood is loosely based on the Grimm Brothers' *Little Red Cap*. The film is directed by Catherine Hardwicke, who directed the first *Twilight* film. Although you may find the film a bit plodding and some of the plot points contrived, you should enjoy some aspects of this version of the fairy tale. *Red Riding Hood* should provide a good starting point to a discussion of household tales and Jungian analysis of household tales.

Synopsis

Valerie (Seyfried) lives in the small village of at an unspecified time in the past, and wears a red cape made for her by her grandmother. Valerie and wood cutter Peter (Fernandez) are in love, but Valerie's parents have arranged for her to marry the wealthier Henry (Irons). The village has an uneasy truce with a werewolf, sacrificing a pig every full moon so the villagers' lives are spared. But the twenty-year-old truce is broken when the wolf kills Valerie's older sister. When the villagers, led by Valerie's father Cesaire (Burke), fail to find the wolf, werewolf expert Father Solomon (Oldman) is called to help. He determines that the werewolf is a member of the village. Valerie suspects Henry, Peter, and even her own grandmother (Christie). The wolf returns, terrorizes the villagers, and corners Valerie and her friend. The wolf speaks to Valerie and calls her by name, telling her that she and the wolf are the same. He says he will return for her. But when Father Solomon learns that Valerie spoke to the wolf, he accuses her of being a witch and jails her, intending to sacrifice her to the wolf. Max and Peter plan to rescue Valerie, but Valerie believes either man could be the wolf. The wolf appears again and asks Valerie to come with him. Valerie escapes and goes to her grandmother's house and finds her grandmother has been killed by the werewolf. Valerie encounters her father, Cesaire, and learns that he is the werewolf. He wants to make Valerie an invincible werewolf like him, but she does not want to be a killer. Peter breaks in to the cabin and fights with Cesaire, but Valerie kills her father the wolf. Valerie and Peter sew rocks into Cesaire's belly and throw his body into the lake. Despite the fact that the wolf has bitten Peter and he will turn into a werewolf at the full moon, Valerie refuses to kill Peter. Peter runs away to learn to control his wolf nature, after consummating his relationship with Valerie. Valerie leaves the village and goes to the forest to wait for Peter's return. When he returns to her as a wolf, she smiles.

Discussion Questions

1. Explain how the film reflects both traditional and contemporary values.

2. Describe how the film shows Valerie's transition from childhood to full adulthood.

3. Explain how the film portrays the ideas of a child's dissatisfaction with parents.

20. Seinfeld, "The Soup"

Film Data

Year: 1994, Season 6, episode 7

Director: Andy Ackerman

Length: 23 minutes

Rated: TV/PG

Characters/Actors

Jerry Seinfeld: Jerry Seinfeld

Elaine Benes: Julia Louis-Dreyfus

Kramer: Michael Richards

George: Jason Alexander

Kenny Bania: Steve Hytner

Connection to Chapters

Chapter 30. Applying Theory: Meals in the Bible (Mary Douglas)

Recommended Scenes

The scene of Kenny offering Jerry the suit occurs at 00:02:26 through 00:03:13.

The scene of Kenny making the deal for the meal occurs at 00:04:45 through 00:05:38.

The scene of Jerry and Kenny having soup and a meal occurs at 00:11:05 through 00:12:08.

The scene of Jerry and Elaine discussing the issue of soup as a meal occurs at 00:12:12 through 00:13:12.

The scene of Jerry, George, and Kenny in the coffee shop occurs at 00:14:08 through 00:15:33.

You may be familiar with the *Seinfeld* series, but even if you are not, you can enjoy the characters and humor. The episode focuses directly on the many meanings of meals and should be an excellent and dynamic way to discuss the concepts of food as code, the social boundaries determined by meals, and the meal as a ritual.

Synopsis

Kenny Bania (Hytner), an annoying acquaintance of Jerry's (Seinfeld), tells Jerry that he has worked out so much that his brand new designer suit doesn't fit him. Kenny offers to give Jerry the suit and Jerry reluctantly agrees. When Kenny drops off the suit to Jerry, Kramer (Richards) comments on Kenny's generosity. Kenny says he does not want anything for the suit, but perhaps Jerry would buy him a meal sometime. Jerry does not want to spend any time with Kenny, but Kenny insists on dinner that evening at a nice restaurant. At the restaurant, Kenny orders soup, saying he is not very hungry and he will save the meal for another time. Jerry wants to count their dinner as the meal, but Kenny insists that soup is not a meal. Later in the episode, Jerry and his friend Elaine (Louis-Dreyfus) discuss the meal. When Kenny runs into Jerry and George at a coffeeshop, he insists on joining them. Kenny asks the waitresses about soup, and Jerry suggests that Kenny order a sandwich. Kenny orders soup and a sandwich. Jerry says this counts as the meal owed, but Kenny disagrees. Disgusted by the whole incident, Jerry gives the designer suit to Elaine's boyfriend.

Discussion Questions

1. **Explain how the episode portrays the idea of food as a code.**

2. **Describe how the episode shows the social boundaries determined by the food meanings.**

3. **Describe how the episode portrays meals as the line between intimacy and distance.**

21. Serenity

Film Data

Year: 2005

Director: Joss Whedon

Length: 119 minutes

Rated: PG-13

Characters/Actors

Nathan Fillion:	Mal
Gina Torres:	Zoë
Alan Tudyk:	Wash
Morena Baccarin:	Inara
Adam Baldwin:	Jayne
Jewel Staite:	Kaylee
Sean Maher:	Simon
Summer Glau:	River
Ron Glass:	Shepherd Derrial Book
Chiwetel Ejiofor:	The Operative

Connection to Chapters

Chapter 41. *Stagecoach* and *Firefly:* The Journey into the Unknown in Westerns and Science Fiction

Recommended Scenes

The scene of River's teacher explaining the history of the Alliance occurs at the start of the film through 00:02:13.

The scene of the Operator asking Mal to settle things like civilized men occurs at 00:53:40.

The scene of Shepherd's death and the Operator justifying his actions occurs at 01:05:40 through 01:09:09.

The scene of Mal threatening to shoot his crew if they do not help him occurs at 01:10:17.

The scene of the crew watching the video explanation of the experiment on Miranda occurs at 01:18:04 through 01:20:01.

The scene of Mal telling his crew that someone needs to speak for the people harmed occurs at 01:20:45 through 01:22:38.

The scene of River defeating the Reavers, Mal battling the Operator, and the resolution of the story occurs at 01:41:49 through the end of the film.

Viewing Information

Serenity continues the story of the cult television series *Firefly*. The film also provides background and explanations for some of the plot points raised in the series. If you are not familiar with the series or the film, you should still be able to understand the plot. *Serenity* should provide an excellent way to discuss the role of science fiction in mythology and to examine the way the film reflects the concerns of its audience.

Synopsis

Serenity takes place 500 years in the future in a solar system governed by an interplanetary body called the Alliance. Captain Mal (Fillion) and his crew—Zoë (Torres), Wash (Tudyk), Jayne (Baldwin), and Kaylee (Staite)—eke out a living on their cargo ship Serenity. They also hide a brother and sister, Simon (Maher) and River (Glau), from the Alliance. River was part of an Alliance experiment and is now unstable. The Alliance has been chasing River ever since Simon freed her. The situation has become more serious, and Mal elects to let the sibling stay. The Alliance is using a deadly and persistent agent known as The Operative (Ejiofor) to capture and kill River. While running from the Alliance, the Serenity crew must also contend with the vicious Reavers. The crew finally learns that the Alliance performed an experiment on the planet Miranda that made the population too docile to live. However, a small part of that population became vicious killers called the Reavers. River knows this secret and is a threat to the Alliance. Mal and his crew find video evidence of this and risk their lives to broadcast this message. Wash is killed, Simon and Kaylee are wounded, and River kills the attacking Reavers. Mal wounds the Operator and broadcasts the tape. When the Operator learns the truth about the Alliance, he prevents its soldiers from killing Mal and his crew. The film ends with Mal and his crew continuing on, with River as copilot. They have damaged the Alliance and are safe for now.

Discussion Questions

1. **Explain how the film explores the idea of individualism and the group.**

2. **Explain the film's underlying assumptions about civilization.**

3. **Describe the film's underlying assumptions about civilization and alternate communities.**

4. **Describe the film's underlying assumptions about the government and science.**

22. Sita Sings the Blues

Film Data

Year: 2008

Director: Nina Paley

Length: 82 minutes

Rated: N/A

Characters/Actors

Annette Hanshaw: Sita (singing) (archive sound)

Aseem Chhabra: Narrator, Shadow Puppet 1 (voice)

Bhavana Nagulapally: Narrator, Shadow Puppet 2 (voice)

Manish Acharya: Narrator, Shadow Puppet 3 (voice)

Reena Shah: Sita (voice)

Sanjiv Jhaveri: Dave/Dasharatha/Ravana/Dhobi/Valmiki (voice)

Debargo Sanyal: Rama (voice)

Nina Paley: Nina (voice)

Connection to Chapters

Chapter 18. India: The *Ramayana*

Recommended Scenes

The scene of Ravana kidnapping Sita occurs at 00:17:01 through 00:22:00.

The scene of Sita refusing to give in to Ravana and the narrators commenting on Sita's actions occurs at 00:27:33 through 00:31:34.

The scene of Sita's kidnapping and Ravana's proposal occurs at 00:17:17 through 00:24:01.

The scene of Sita's rescue, Rama's rejection and the test of the funeral pyre of occurs at 00:37:21 through 00:42:51.

The scene of Sita and Rama forgiving each other occurs at 00:43:27.

The scene of the Indian dance occurs at 00:51:05 through 00:54:26

The scene of Sita's sons learning songs of praise for Rama occurs at 01:04:43 through 01:06:25.

The final scene of Sita being taken into the womb of mother earth begins at 01:10:59.

Viewing Information

Although the credits for this animated musical say that it is based on the *Ramayana* by Valmiki, *Sita Sings the Blues* includes some Western elements. The film is in English and uses songs by 1920's jazz vocalist Annette Hanshaw to emphasize Sita's emotions throughout the story. Interspersed with the story of Sita (Shah) and Rama (Sanyal) is a modern tale of Dave (Jhaveri) and Nina (Paley), who live in San Francisco with their cat, but eventually break up. The film also uses three narrators (Chhabra, Nagulapally, and Acharya) with Indian accents who tell the story of Sita by piecing together what they remember of the story, commenting on the story and offering their opinions. This charming and vibrant film is an excellent way to begin a discussion of the *Ramayana,* the concept of *dharma,* and the resonance of this myth in present times.

Synopsis

The film focuses on the part of the *Ramayana* that relates to Sita's kidnapping and rescue by Rama. Rama agrees to be banished for fourteen years to the forest, and his wife Sita insists on accompanying him. Ravana (Jhaveri) is persuaded to use trickery to kidnap Sita. He proposes marriage to Sita and threatens her with death if she refuses. He gives her two months to decide, but Sita remains true to Rama. Rama rescues Sita, but then he rejects her, saying she must have been defiled during the time she was kidnapped. Sita asks for the funeral pyre to prove her purity. She is rescued by the gods, and Rama and Sita reunite. However, later Rama says that his subjects do not respect him because of Sita, and he banishes Sita. A pregnant Sita goes to the forest and gives birth to twin boys. Rama finds them many years later and welcomes his sons back to the kingdom. However, Rama asks Sita to prove her purity again. Sita agrees and says that if she is completely pure, mother earth should take her back into her womb. The film ends when Sita is taken back into the womb of mother earth. Sita sings and Rama sheds a tear.

1. **Describe how the characters in the film illustrate the concept of *dharma*.**

2. **Explain how the film shows how the Hindu gods take a personal interest in the lives of humans.**

3. **Describe how the film incorporates Indian traditions surrounding the myth.**

23. Stagecoach

Film Data

Year: 1939

Director: John Ford

Length: 96 minutes

Rated: N/A

Characters/Actors

Claire Trevor: Dallas

John Wayne: Ringo Kid

Andy Devine: Buck

John Carradine: Hatfield

Thomas Mitchell: Doc Boone

Louise Platt: Lucy Mallory

George Bancroft: Curley

Donald Meek: Peacock

Berton Churchill: Gatewood

Connection to Chapters

Chapter 41. *Stagecoach* and *Firefly:* The Journey into the Unknown in Westerns and Science Fiction

Recommended Scenes

The scene of the Law and Order League occurs at 00:06:49.

The scene of the group voting to keep going occurs at 00:25:58.

The scene of the group cooing over Lucy's baby occurs at 00:48:34 through 00:49:56.

The scene of Doc Boone toasting the group occurs at 01:10:20.

The scene of the battle with the Apaches and the ensuing rescue by the army occurs at 01:10:23 through 01:17:10.

The scene of Curley and the doctor letting Ringo and Dallas get away occurs at 01:33:49 through the end of the film.

Viewing Information

The acclaimed *Stagecoach* is a black-and-white Western directed by John Ford. While the fight sequences look much different than those in more contemporary films, the action sequences remain raw and exciting. *Stagecoach* provides excellent examples of the travelers as family, community, morality, and the journey fraught with peril. The timeless themes present in this excellent film should provide the framework for a lively discussion of this Western's influence on science fiction.

Synopsis

Stagecoach chronicles the journey of six passengers and their drivers from the town of Tonto to Lordsburg. The stagecoach is driven by Buck (Devine) and lawman Curley (Bancroft), who goes along to look for fugitive Ringo (Wayne). The passengers include prostitute Dallas (Trevor) and drunken Doc Boone (Mitchell). Both have been thrown out of town by the Law and Order League. Corrupt banker Gatewood (Churchill), whiskey salesman Peacock (Meek), gambler Hatfield (Carradine), and pregnant Lucy (Platt), who travels to meet her husband, make up the rest of the passenger list. The group soon picks up escaped prisoner Ringo. Curley intends to arrest Ringo, but Ringo's skills are needed on the journey. Along the way, the passengers get to know and care about each other, all help Lucy deliver her baby, and Ringo and Dallas fall in love. The group fights off attacking Apaches and Hatfield is killed. The rest of the group arrives safely in Lordsburg. Ringo settles a score with two brothers who wronged him and agrees to return to jail. Dallas says she will marry Ringo. As the film ends, it appears Curley will allow Ringo to escape to his ranch for a life with Dallas.

Discussion Questions

1. Explain how the film questions conventional ideas of morality.

2. Describe the film's underlying assumptions about civilization and alternate communities.

3. Describe the film's underlying assumptions about the military.

24. Star Trek II: The Wrath of Khan

Film Data

Year: 1982

Director: Nicholas Meyer

Length: 113 minutes

Rated: PG

Characters/Actors

William Shatner: Admiral James T. Kirk

Leonard Nimoy: Captain Spock

DeForest Kelley: Dr. McCoy

Kirstie Alley: Lt. Saavik

Ricardo Montalban: Khan

Bibi Besch: Dr. Carol Marcus

Merritt Butrick: Dr. David Marcus

Walter Koenig: Mr. Chekov

Connection to Chapters

Chapter 41. *Stagecoach* and *Firefly:* The Journey into the Unknown in Westerns and Science Fiction

Recommended Scenes

The scene of Chekov discussing the genetic engineering experiment occurs at 00:18:11.

The scene of Spock talking to Kirk about the needs of the many and Kirk's destiny occurs at 00:39:22 through 00:40:11.

The scene of Dr. Marcus explaining Project Genesis and the ensuing debate about it occurs at 00:43:20 through 00:46:04.

The scene of the start of the battle between Khan and Kirk begins at 00:51:07.

The scene of Khan trying to detonate Project Genesis occurs at 01:30:12.

The scene of Spock sacrificing himself and his farewell to Kirk occurs at 01:31:48 through 01:39:12.

The scene of Spock's funeral and the resolution of the story occur at 01:39:41 through the end of the film.

Viewing Information

The original *Star Trek* series ran from 1966 through 1969. The series spawned other television series, as well as eleven films between 1979 through 2009. *Star Trek II: The Wrath of Khan* features the cast and characters from the original series, as well Khan (Montalban), a villain from a past series episode. *Star Trek II: The Wrath of Khan* is an excellent way to begin a discussion of science fiction and myth. The film also provides rich examples of the changing values of the group, the individual, and science, and should lead to a vibrant discussion.

Synopsis

The film begins with a training simulation involving members of the former crew of the starship *Enterprise* and new recruits. But problems force Admiral Kirk (Shatner) to take control of the ship and investigate, using both his old crew and the recruits. Another starship has encountered Kirk's old enemy Khan. Khan is ruthless in his attempt to steal Project Genesis, a life-generating technology developed by Kirk's old flame Dr. Marcus (Besch) and her son David (Butrick), who is later revealed to be Kirk's son. Khan also wants to get revenge on Kirk. A battle ensues. The battle with Khan allows old friends Kirk, Spock (Nimoy) and McCoy (Kelley) to explore their feelings about their life choices, growing older, and their enduring friendships. Both McCoy and Spock believe that Kirk should return to being a captain. As the space battle continues, Kirk manages to outmaneuver Khan and defeat him. But Khan has obtained Project Genesis and uses it as a weapon to try to destroy the *Enterprise*. The *Enterprise* suffers losses, and it appears Project Genesis will detonate and destroy the ship. Spock prevents this by sacrificing his life. After Spock's funeral, Kirk and the crew send Spock's remains to a planet being regenerated by Project Genesis. At the end of the film, Kirk states that he hopes to return to that planet soon. Kirk says that he feels young again, and sees life's many possibilities.

Discussion Questions

1. Explain how the film reflects the audience's attitudes about science.

2. Describe the film's underlying assumptions about religion.

3. Explain how the film portrays the values of the group over the values of the individual.

4. Describe the film's underlying assumptions about the place of human beings in the cosmos.

25. Star Wars Episode Four: A New Hope

Film Data

Year: 1977

Director: George Lucas

Length: 121 minutes

Rated: PG

Characters/Actors

Mark Hamill: Luke Skywalker

Harrison Ford: Han Solo

Carrie Fisher: Princess Leia Organa

Anthony Daniels: C-3P0

Alec Guinness: Ben Obi-Wan Kenobi

Kenny Baker   R2-D2

David Prowse   Darth Vader

James Earl Jones   Darth Vader (voice)

Connection to Chapters

Chapter 15. Theory: Joseph Campbell, *The Hero with a Thousand Faces* (Dave Whomsley)

Recommended Scenes

The scene of Luke's initial conversation with the androids and the message from Princess Leia occurs at 00:20:51 through 00:22:57.

The scene of the first conversation between Ben and Luke occurs at 00:31:09 through 00:36:32.

The scene in the Mos Eisley bar occurs at 00:43:35.

The scene of Luke receiving Jedi training from Ben occurs at 00:58:20.

The scene of Luke, Han, and Leia trapped in the "belly of the whale" occurs at 01:17:01.

The scene of the light saber battle between Ben and Darth Vader occurs at 01:27:35.

The scene of Han refusing to join Luke and Luke discussing it with Leia occurs at 01:39:00 through 01:40:22.

The scene of the last part of the battle and the resolution occurs at 01:51:00 through the end of the film.

Viewing Information

The 1977 *Star Wars* was the first film in a series of six. To date, the last film was released in 2005. The most recent three films were prequels. *Episode IV: A New Hope* was later added to the title of the 1977 *Star Wars*. *Star Wars* is an excellent way to discuss Joseph Campbell's ideas, especially because of the direct influence of Campbell on George Lucas' work. This film will provide a good way to illustrate the hero cycle described by Campbell.

Synopsis

The film takes place at unspecified time in the future when space travel is common. The film opens with a written introduction on the screen explaining that there is a civil war against the ruling galactic empire. Working with the empire, Darth Vader (Prowse/Jones) kidnaps Princess Leia (Fisher) in an attempt to steal plans for a lethal weapon. Aspiring pilot Luke Skywalker (Hamill) has the job of taking care of two androids, R2-D2 (Baker) and C-3P0 (Daniels). While working on them, he finds an old video message from Princess Leia asking for help from Ben Obi-Wan Kenobi (Guinness). When Luke finds Ben Kenobi, he learns about his father, a Jedi knight, and is given his father's weapon, the light saber. Luke joins Ben on the mission to help rescue Princess Leia. Ben trains Luke and they recruit a mercenary pilot, Han Solo (Ford), to help them. Together they rescue Princess Leia and battle the empire. Ben lets Darth Vader kill him, knowing that Luke will continue the fight. During the final battle, Han Solo helps Luke Skywalker defeat the empire forces. The film ends with Princess Leia giving Luke and Han medals.

Discussion Questions

1. Describe how Luke Skywalker follows the steps in the hero's journey as outlined by Joseph Campbell.

2. Describe how Han Solo follows the steps in the hero's journey as outlined by Joseph Campbell.

3. Explain the role destiny and free will play in the lives of the characters.

26. Tangled

Film Data

Year: 2010

Director: Nathan Greno and Byron Howard

Length: 100 minutes

Rated: PG

Characters/Actors

Rapunzel (voice):   Mandy Moore

Flynn Rider (voice):   Zachary Levi

Mother Gothel (voice):   Donna Murphy

Stabbington Brother (voice): Ron Perlman

Captain of the Guard (voice): M. C. Gainey

Big Nose Thug (voice):   Jeffrey Tambor

Hook Hand Thug (voice) :   Brad Garrett

Connection to Chapters

Chapter 34. Applying Theory: How to Perform a Jungian Analysis

Chapter 37. Germany: Grimms' *Household Tales*

Recommended Scenes

The scene of Mother Gothel singing about why Rapunzel cannot ever leave occurs at 00:13:04 through 00:15:35.

The scene of Mother Gothel and Rapunzel hugging occurs at 00:24:20.

The scene of Rapunzel making the deal with Flynn and then singing about seeing the world occurs at 00:28:31 through 00:30:28.

The scene of Rapunzel realizing her dream and seeing the lanterns occurs at 01:06:42.

The scene of the final confrontation between Rapunzel and Mother Gothel occurs from 01:15:30 through 01:19:00.

The scene of Flynn cutting Rapunzel's hair and then being healed by her tears occurs at 01:24:30.

The scene of Rapunzel being reunited with her real parents and living happily ever after occurs at 01:28:47.

Viewing Information

Tangled is very loosely based on the Grimm Brothers' *Rapunzel,* even though the film gives Jacob and Wilhelm Grimm a screenwriting credit along with Dan Fogelman. *Tangled* is a Disney musical with music composed by Alan Menken. The film's characters are voiced by pop star Mandy Moore, Broadway star Donna Murphy, and television star Zach Levi. *Tangled* should be a good way to discuss Otto Rank's ideas about the family romance, as well as a good way to start a discussion of household tales and Jungian analysis of household tales.

Synopsis

Mother Gothel (Murphy) finds a magical flower with healing powers. She uses it to keep herself young. Later, the flower is found to heal a Queen who is ill and in childbirth. The Queen gives birth to Rapunzel (Moore), whose hair glows and heals, but will lose its magic if cut. Mother Gothel kidnaps the baby and raises Rapunzel as her daughter. She never cuts Rapunzel's hair and keeps her locked from the world in a tower. Every year on her birthday, the King and Queen release lanterns of light, hoping the lost princess will return. Rapunzel watches the lights and wants to see them on her eighteenth birthday. The Queen refuses. When a thief named Flynn (Levi) steals a tiara from the castle, he hides in the tower. Rapunzel hits him with a frying pan and gets the tiara. She makes a deal with Flynn to exchange the tiara for a chance to see the lights. They escape, have adventures, and begin to have romantic feelings for each other. Eventually Gothel captures Rapunzel and Flynn. Rapunzel realizes that she is the real princess and that Gothel kidnapped her. She says that if Gothel spares Flynn's life, she will stay with Gothel forever. Before Rapunzel can heal Flynn with her hair, Flynn cuts it. Gothel grows old and dies and Rapunzel heals Flynn. Rapunzel is reunited with her parents and takes her rightful place as the princess. She marries Flynn, and all live happily in the kingdom.

1. Explain how the film illustrates the maturation and initiation cycle, as well as Rank's ideas of the family romance.

2. Explain how the film changes the tale to reflect contemporary values.

3. Describe how the film portrays changing ideas of parent/child relationships.

27. Thor

Film Data

Year: 2011

Director: Kenneth Branagh

Length: 115 minutes

Rated: PG-13

Characters/Actors

Chris Hemsworth:	Thor
Natalie Portman:	Jane Foster
Tom Hiddleston:	Loki
Anthony Hopkins:	Odin
Stellan Skarsgård:	Erik Selvig
Kat Dennings:	Darcy Lewis
Clark Gregg:	Agent Coulson
Idris Elba:	Heimdall
Colm Feore:	King Laufey

Connection to Chapters

Chapter 19. Icelandic/Norse: *Prose Edda*

Chapter 31. Icelandic/Norse: The Rituals of Iceland (H. R. E. Davidson)

Recommended Scenes

The scene of Odin telling Thor he is thinking like a warrior occurs at 00:012:15.

The scene of Loki and Thor battling the frost giants occurs at 00:17:36 through 00:22:28.

The scene of Odin banishing Thor occurs at 00:26:28 through 00:29:41.

The scene of the gods talking about Loki being mischievous occurs at 00:39:04.

The scene of Thor trying to retrieve his hammer at the military facility occurs at 00:54:43 through 00:58:40.

The scene of Loki lying to Thor on earth occurs at 01:04:43.

The scene of Thor asking Loki to spare innocent lives and then retrieving his hammer and fighting the metal giant occurs at 01:25:00 through 01:29:41.

The scene of the final battle between Thor and Loki occurs at 01:36:00.

Viewing Information

Thor is based on the Marvel comic book by Stan Lee. The film imagines the attractive and strong Thor (Hemsworth) to be somewhat of a superhero, who is banished to earth from Asgard. The film alternates scenes in Asgard with scenes on modern-day earth. Thor is also treated with humor in the scenes on earth. Although the film changes many aspects of the myth of Thor, *Thor* provides some good examples of Thor's better-known characteristics. *Thor* should provide an enjoyable way to discuss the Thor, Odin, Loki, Asgard, and the Norse gods.

Synopsis

Thor is expelled from Asgard by Odin (Hopkins), in part due to the trickery of Loki (Hiddleston). Thor crashes to earth and is found by scientists Jane (Portman), Erik (Skarsgård), and Darcy (Dennings). Thor is now human. Jane helps Thor in his quest to retrieve his hammer, the Mjollnir, and wants Thor to help with her research. The two develop romantic feelings for each other. On Asgard, Loki's machinations place him in charge while Odin is seriously ill. Loki attempts to strand Thor on earth and sends a metal giant to kill him. Thor fights the giant and retrieves his hammer and saves Jane and the other humans. Thor learns the truth about Loki and is able to return to Asgard. Odin is saved and Thor saves the frost giants from Loki's plan to destroy them. But in doing so, Thor must destroy the Bifrost Bridge, which is also the bridge to earth. Thor and Loki fight, and Loki falls to earth. The film ends with reconciliation between Odin and Thor, and Thor is made ruler. Thor misses Jane, but is told that on earth, Jane continues to search for him.

Discussion Questions

1. Explain how the film portrays the transcendence and immanence of Odin and Thor.

2. Describe how the film shows Thor to be both fallible and heroic.

3. Describe how the film portrays Loki as a trickster.

28. *The Tree of Life*

Film Data

Year: 2011

Director: Terrence Malick

Length: 139 minutes

Rated: PG-13

Characters/Actors

Brad Pitt: Mr. O'Brien

Sean Penn: Jack

Jessica Chastain: Mrs. O'Brien

Hunter McCracken: Young Jack

Laramie Eppler: R.L.

Tye Sheridan: Steve

Connection to Chapters

Part IIA. Myths of Creation and Destruction—Creation: Introductory Overview

Chapter 5. The Bible: Genesis (Creation)

Recommended Scenes

The scene of Mrs. O'Brien talking about nature and grace occurs at 00:02:05 through 00:04:14.

The scene of the creation of the world occurs at 00:19:39 through 00:36:59.

The scene of Mr. O'Brien giving his sons advice occurs at 00:59:55 through 01:01:11.

The scene of the end of time and the characters walking together on the beach occurs at 02:01:50 through 02:11:59.

The Tree of Life mixes pensive meditations on the meaning of life with scenes of a 1950s childhood, interwoven with scenes of the creation and destruction of the world. The film is visually stunning, and tells some of its story with little accompanying dialogue. The film features excellent performances from actors Brad Pitt and Sean Penn. *The Tree of Life* should provide an interesting way to discuss creation and the relevance of creation myths for contemporary audiences.

Synopsis

The film begins with young Mrs. O'Brien (Chastain) learning that her nineteen-year-old son has been killed. Neighbors offer the grieving parents sympathy. The scene then shifts to middle-aged Jack O'Brien (Penn) in his successful job in a high-rise building. He seems unhappy as he thinks about his dead brother and his childhood. Most of the film recounts scenes from Jack's childhood in suburban Texans in the 1950s. Young Jack (McCracken) and his brothers R.L. (Eppler) and Steve (Sheridan) spend long days playing outside. They sometimes hear their parents argue through open windows. Their mother is loving and sweet, but their father, Mr. O'Brien (Pitt), is strict and sometimes seems abusive. Mr. O'Brien works in a plant, but yearned to be a musician in his youth. He spends his free time patenting and trying to sell his numerous inventions. Jack, who is the oldest brother, misbehaves and frequently clashes with his stern father. Near the end of the film, the plant employing Mr. O'Brien closes and the family sadly leaves their home. Interspersed with the scenes of Jack's childhood are scenes of a pensive adult Jack at home and at work. We also see scenes that appear to show the universe being created. Over some of these scenes are whispered musings from Mrs. O'Brien, young Jack, and the adult Jack. The characters wonder about God, suffering, love and the meaning of the life. The film ends with a vision of an afterlife where adult Jack meets his younger self, his brothers as children, and his parents as they looked in his childhood. They embrace and seem happy, and others join them as they walk together on a beach.

Discussion Questions

1. **Describe the way creation myths are referred to in the film.**

2. **Explain how the film refers to the biblical creation story in Genesis.**

3. Describe how the film uses details of both the character's daily lives and their view of creation to show their priorities.

29. Troy

Film Data

Year: 2004

Director: Wolfgang Petersen

Length: 163 minutes

Rated: R

Characters/Actors

Brad Pitt:	Achilles
Brian Cox:	Agamemnon
Brendan Gleeson:	Menelaus
Diane Kruger:	Helen
Eric Bana:	Hector
Orlando Bloom:	Paris
Peter O'Toole:	Priam
Saffron Burrows:	Andromache
Rose Byrne:	Briseis
Garrett Hedlund:	Patroclus

Connection to Chapters

Chapter 1. What Is Myth?

Chapter 44. Poetry and Myth

Recommended Scenes

The scene of Achilles talking to his mother occurs at 00:24:53 through 00:26:40.

The scene of Achilles desecrating the temple and discussing immortality with Hector occurs at 00:44:13 through 00:48:05.

The scene of Achilles and Briseis discussing the gods occurs at 01:29:30 through 01:31:17.

The scene of the final battle between Hector and Achilles occurs at 01:57:23 through 02:02:33.

The scene of Priam asking Achilles for Hector's corpse occurs at 02:07:33.

The scene of the Trojan horse and ensuing battle begins at 02:17:28.

Viewing Information

Troy is big-budget sprawling adventure and romance film that tells the story of the Trojan War. The film credits Homer along with screenwriter David Benioff for the characters and story. The film provides an interesting way to discuss contemporary film adaptations of myths. *Troy* also provides an interesting and enjoyable way to discuss the role of the gods in the lives of mortals, as well as the importance of immortality for these characters.

Synopsis

While Paris (Bloom) and Hector (Bana) are in Sparta for peace negotiations with King Menelaus (Gleeson), Paris and Helen (Kruger), the king's wife, fall in love. When Paris and Helen leave together, an angry Menelaus and his war-mongering brother King Agamemnon (Cox) prepare to attack Troy. Achilles (Pitt) is Agamemnon's best warrior, but they have a strained relationship. Achilles reluctantly agrees to fight. Troy suffers losses, and Briseis (Byrne), who is cousin to Paris and Hector, is taken prisoner by Achilles. Paris challenges Menelaus to a fight in order to resolve the dispute. Paris does not fight well and loses, but Hector protects his brother by killing Menelaus. Achilles and Briseis develop romantic feelings for each other, and Achilles orders his army to leave Troy. But Achilles' young cousin Patroclus (Hedlund) dresses in Achilles' armor and attacks Troy. Hector kills Patroclus, thinking he is Achilles. An enraged Achilles fights Hector and kills him. Achilles allows King Priam (O'Toole) to bury his son Hector and allows Briseis to return to Troy. Agamemnon's army and Achilles hide in a large model of a horse and burn Troy. Agamemnon threatens Briseis, but Briseis kills him. Achilles then comes to her rescue and helps Briseis escape. Paris then shoots Achilles in the heel and kills him. Achilles and Briseis kiss goodbye as he dies, and then Briseis escapes with Paris and Helen.

Discussion Questions

1. Explain how the characters in the film view human freedom and the role of the gods.

2. Describe how the characters in the film view the importance of eternal fame and mortal lives.

3. Explain how the film interprets the myth to reflect the changing tastes and expectations of a contemporary audience.

30. Twilight

Film Data

Year: 2008

Director: Catherine Hardwicke

Length: 122 minutes

Rated: PG-13

Characters/Actors

Kristen Stewart: Bella Swan

Robert Pattinson: Edward Cullen

Billy Burke: Charlie Swan

Taylor Lautner: Jacob Black

Rachelle Lefevre: Victoria

Peter Facinelli: Dr. Carlisle Cullen

Sarah Clarke: Renée

Cam Gigandet: James

Connection to Chapters

Chapter 43. The Vampire as Hero: Tales of the Undead in a Contemporary Context

Recommended Scenes

The scene of Edward stopping a car from hitting Bella occurs at 00:21:13.

The scene of Edward rescuing Bella from a gang of predatory boys and then telling Bella he feels protective toward her occurs at 00:39:38 through 00:44:30.

The scene of Bella and Edward discussing his vampire urges and self-control occurs at 00:50:20 through 00:56:05.

The scene of Edward telling Bella about the temptation of human blood occurs at 00:59:47.

The scene Edward stopping himself from having sex with Bella occurs at 01:15:01 through 01:16:09.

The scene of Carlisle telling his family to protect Bella occurs at 01:30:08.

The scene of Edward sucking the venom from Bella's blood occurs at 01:45:00.

Viewing Information

Twilight is the first in the series of films based on Stephenie Meyer's best-selling novels. Although the film continues with the conservative ideologies found in the novels, *Twilight* provides a good way to begin a discussion of vampires. *Twilight* provides an excellent way to examine the reasons for the popularity of vampires, the ideas of Melanie Klein and the values advanced in this film.

Synopsis

When her mother Renée (Clarke) goes on the road with her husband, Bella (Stewart), a high school student, moves to Forks, Washington, to live with her father, Charlie (Burke). Moping Bella meets fellow student Edward Cullen (Pattinson) and although he pretends to dislike her, their mutual attraction is obvious. Edward displays unusual strength when he pushes Bella out of the path of an oncoming car and saves her from attack by a gang of predatory boys. Bella realizes that something is not right with Edward and his mysterious family, but does not figure out that he is a vampire until halfway through the film. Edward tells her that he and his family only eat animals, but he is tempted by Bella's blood, and cannot trust himself to get too close to her. But they begin to date and Edward introduces Bella to his family. They encounter another clan of vampires who have been killing people in Forks. These vampires are led by Victoria (Lefevre) and James (Gigandet). When tracker James gets Bella's scent, Bella must leave town. Edward's family helps her, but James threatens Bella's mother and captures Bella. Edward and his family come to the rescue and save Bella's life. Bella recovers from her injuries and tells her mother she wants to remain in Forks with her father. The film ends with Edward and Bella at the prom. Bella wants Edward to turn her into a vampire so they can be together forever. Edward refuses for now, and the film ends with the couple dancing.

Discussion Questions

1. Explain how the film shows Melanie Klein's ideas about "inappropriate mothering."

2. Describe how the film portrays men and women struggling with greedy and powerful aspects of their world and their own nature.

3. Explain how the film shows that Bella's encounters with vampires allow her to reshape her world.

31. Whale Rider

Film Data

Year: 2002

Director: Niki Caro

Length: 101 minutes

Rated: PG-13

Characters/Actors

Keisha Castle-Hughes: Paikea

Rawiri Paratene: Koro

Vicky Haughton: Nanny Flowers

Cliff Curtis: Porourangi

Grant Roa: Uncle Rawiri

Connection to Chapters

Chapter 15. Theory: Joseph Campbell, *The Hero with a Thousand Faces* (Dave Whomsley)

Chapter 34. Applying Theory: How to Perform a Jungian Analysis

Recommended Scenes

The scene of Koro and Porourangi arguing about the obligations of destiny occurs at 00:22:11 through 00:24:10.

The scene of Porourangi explaining Koro and traditions to Pai occurs at 00:25:30 through 00:27:16.

The scene of Uncle Rawiri training Pai occurs at 00:46:20 through 00:47:40.

The scene of Pai giving a speech about her grandfather occurs at 01:11:40 through 01:15:48.

The scene of Pai riding the whale occurs at 01:25:38 through 01:31:40.

The scene of Koro accepting Pai, the ceremony, and the resolution of the story occurs at 01:33:20 through the end of the film.

Viewing Information

Whale Rider was shot on the New Zealand island where it takes places. The film features a much-acclaimed performance from then-eleven-year-old Keisha Castle-Hughes. While this film is about a child, this is not a children's film. *Whale Rider* provides an excellent example of a young girl on a hero's quest. The film should also provide an enjoyable and interesting way to discuss the ideas of Joseph Campbell, as well as Jung's archetypes. *Whale Rider* tells a story of the relevance of old myths to a present day culture, and should start an interesting discussion.

Synopsis

The film is set in present-day New Zealand. A flashback voiced by young Pai (Castle-Hughes) tells us that Pai's mother died in childbirth, as did her twin brother. Pai is descended from a line of Maori chiefs, dating back to the first ancestor Paikea. Legend has it that Paikea rode on a whale from another island. The title of chief is passed through first born sons, and Pai's dead brother was thought to be the next in line after Pai's father. Overcome with sadness, Pai's father, Porourani (Curtis), leaves the island to be an artist. He does not wish to be the next chief, even though he would be next in line. Pai is raised by her grandmother Nanny Flowers (Haughton) and her grandfather Koro (Paratene). They love her, but Koro wishes she were a boy. When Koro feels the village needs a new chief, he trains all the firstborn boys in the old ways. Pai wants to attend but it is forbidden for girls. She spies and learns on her own, and shows both aptitude and passion. Pai angers Koro, but she continues to love him. Pai turns down the chance to leave with her father because she feels she must stay in her village. Signs point to Pai as the new chief, but Koro refuses to believe the new chief could be a girl. When Pai risks her life by riding a beached whale to sea, Koro finally accepts her as the new leader. The film ends with the entire village, including the returning Porourangi, happily celebrating together in a colorful religious ceremony. Pai has unified all in the village. In a voiceover she stated that she knows her people will continue on.

Discussion Questions

1. **Explain how in the film Pai takes some of the steps in the hero's journey as outlined by Campbell.**

2. **Describe how Pai's journey in the film is a spiritual quest.**

3. **Describe how the film uses Jung's archetypes of animus, shadow, and self.**

32. The Wizard of Oz

Film Data

Year: 1939

Director: Victor Fleming

Length: 101 minutes

Rated: N/A

Characters/Actors

Judy Garland:	Dorothy Gale
Frank Morgan:	Professor Marvel/The Wizard of Oz/The Gatekeeper/The Carriage Driver/The Guard
Ray Bolger:	Hunk/The Scarecrow
Bert Lahr:	Zeke/The Cowardly Lion
Jack Haley:	Hickory/The Tin Man
Billie Burke:	Glinda
Margaret Hamilton:	Miss Gulch/The Wicked Witch of the West
Clara Blandick:	Auntie Em

Connection to Chapters

Chapter 36. Applying Theory: A Proppian Analysis of *The Wizard of Oz*

Recommended Scenes

The opening scene of Dorothy discussing her problems, singing, and battling Miss Gulch occurs at 00:02:49 through 00:10:44.

The scene of the tornado occurs at 00:15:52 through 00:19:11.

The scenes in Oz occur from 00:19:30 through 01:39:12.

The scene of Dorothy encountering Glinda and The Wicked Witch occurs at 00:21:32 though 00:31:04.

The scene of Dorothy meeting the Scarecrow, Tin Man, and Lion occurs at 00:34:14 through 00:53:10.

The scene of the final battle with the Wicked Witch and her eventual destruction occurs at 01:15:45 through 01:27:13.

The scene Dorothy exposing the Wizard occurs at 01:28:24.

The scenes in Kansas resolving the story occur from 01:39:12 through the end of the film.

Viewing Information

The Wizard of Oz is a well-known musical featuring black-and-white and color scenes. The film provides an enjoyable and interesting way to discuss rationalization of myths, changing audiences, and gender roles in myth. Those familiar with *The Wizard of Oz* as children will be able to examine the film with new insights and appreciation. *The Wizard of Oz* also provides a good way to introduce Proppian analysis.

Synopsis

Dorothy (Garland) lives on a Kansas farm with her Aunt Em (Blandick), Uncle Henry (Grapewin), and farm hands Hunk (Bolger), Zeke (Lahr), and Hickory (Haley). After mean Miss Gulch (Hamilton) takes away Dorothy's dog Toto, Toto escapes and Dorothy and Toto run away together. An encounter with traveling performer Professor Marvel (Morgan) convinces Dorothy to return home, but by then a tornado has hit the farm. Dorothy is knocked down by a broken window and collapses on her bed. When Dorothy awakens, she believes her house is being carried away by a tornado. She finds herself in the magical Land of Oz, where her house has flattened a witch with ruby slippers. She encounters good witch Glinda (Burke) and The Wicked Witch of the West (Hamilton). Dorothy spends her time in Oz trying to find a way to return home. Glinda gives Dorothy the magic ruby slippers and advises her to see the Wizard of Oz (Morgan). Dorothy is joined on her journey by the Scarecrow (Bolger) seeking a brain, the Tin man (Haley) seeking a heart, and the Lion (Lahr) seeking courage. Dorothy accidentally kills The Wicked Witch and then exposes the wizard as a well-intentioned fraud. The Wizard grants the requests of the group, but Dorothy needs the help of Glinda to return home. Glinda shows Dorothy that she always had the power to return home. When Dorothy opens her eyes, she is back in Kansas, surrounded by her aunt, uncle, and the three farm hands. Dorothy is told she had a dream, but she believes it was real. At the end of the film, Dorothy finds the most important part of her experience was her appreciation for home.

Discussion Questions

1. Explain how the film reflects concern for gender equality.

2. Describe how the filmmakers used the rationalization process to make the film acceptable for adult audiences.

3. Explain how the film's incomplete ending is consistent with the idea that the overall effect is more important than resolving every problem in the tale.

33. *The X-Files,* "The Erlenmeyer Flask"

Film Data

Year: 1994, Season 1, episode 23

Director: R. W. Goodwin

Length: 45 minutes

Rated: TV/14

Characters/Actors

David Duchovny:	Fox Mulder
Gillian Anderson:	Dana Scully
Lindsey Ginter:	Crew Cut Man
Anne De Salvo:	Dr. Anne Carpenter (as Anne DeSalvo)
Simon Webb:	Dr. William Secare
Ken Kramer:	Dr. Terrance Allen Berube
Jerry Hardin:	Deep Throat

Connection to Chapters

Chapter 34. Applying Theory: How to Perform a Jungian Analysis

Chapter 41. *Stagecoach* and *Firefly:* The Journey into the Unknown in Westerns and Science Fiction

Recommended Scenes

The scene of Mulder and Deep Throat arguing about trust occurs at 00:11:02.

The scene of Mulder discovering the lab with tanks of people underwater occurs at 00:22:30.

The scene of Scully finding out about the extra terrestrial DNA occurs at 00:25:01.

The scene of Scully telling Mulder that she always held science sacred occurs at 00:27:25.

The scene of Deep Throat explaining the details of the experiment to Mulder and Scully occurs at 00:28:10 through 00:31:02.

The scene of the exchange, Deep Throat being shot, and the resolution of the story occurs at 00:41:48 through the end of the episode.

Viewing Information

The X-Files ran for nine seasons on television, from 1993 through 2002. FBI agents Fox Mulder (Duchovny) and Dana Scully (Anderson) investigate unsolved cases that may involve paranormal activity. "The Erlenmeyer Flask" is the last episode of the first season. *The X-Files* provides a good way to discuss how science, technology, government, and the individual are viewed in our current society. This episode also provides a good illustration of how popular entertainment reflects the concerns of its audience.

Synopsis

Agent Mulder gets a tip from his source, Deep Throat (Hardin), to investigate a police chase shown on a television news report. Mulder and Scully find a scientist, Dr. Terrance Allen Berube (Kramer), who is doing experiments on animals. The scientist ends up dead, and Mulder and Scully find that he was experimenting with extraterrestrial DNA. One of the subjects, Dr. William Secare (Webb), can now breathe underwater. He is also murdered. Eventually Mulder and Scully find a lab full of tanks with human beings breathing underwater. Deep Throat tells them that this is part of a secret government project. When Mulder is kidnapped, probably by government agents, Deep Throat brokers a deal for Mulder's release. Scully retrieves a flask containing what looks to be a hybrid human fetus and reluctantly gives it to Deep Throat to exchange for Mulder. During the exchange, an injured Mulder is returned and Deep Throat is shot. The episode ends with a recovered Mulder telling Scully that they have been reassigned, but he will continue searching for the truth. The final shot of the episode shows a jar containing the hybrid life form being placed in a file on the shelf of a room in the Pentagon.

Discussion Questions

1. **Explain how the episode shows the series' underlying assumptions about science and technology.**

2. Describe how the episode reflects the concerns of the audience about government and the military.

3. Explain how the characters in the episode view the importance of the individual over the group.